ALSO BY MARTÍN ESPADA

POETRY

Floaters

Vivas to Those Who Have Failed

The Meaning of the Shovel

The Trouble Ball

Soldados en el Jardín

La Tumba de Buenaventura Roig

Crucifixion in the Plaza de Armas

The Republic of Poetry

Alabanza: New and Selected Poems (1982–2002)

A Mayan Astronomer in Hell's Kitchen

Imagine the Angels of Bread

City of Coughing and Dead Radiators

Rebellion Is the Circle of a Lover's Hands

Trumpets from the Islands of Their Eviction

The Immigrant Iceboy's Bolero

TRANSLATION

The Blood That Keeps Singing: Selected Poems of Clemente Soto Vélez
(with Camilo Pérez-Bustillo)

EDITOR

What Saves Us: Poems of Empathy and Outrage in the Age of Trump

His Hands Were Gentle: Selected Lyrics of Víctor Jara

El Coro: A Chorus of Latino and Latina Poetry

Poetry Like Bread: Poets of the Political Imagination from Curbstone Press

ESSAYS

The Lover of a Subversive Is Also a Subversive

Zapata's Disciple

JAILBREAK *of* SPARROWS

JAILBREAK *of* SPARROWS

Poems

Martín Espada

ALFRED A. KNOPF ◆ NEW YORK ◆ 2025

A BORZOI BOOK

FIRST HARDCOVER EDITION PUBLISHED BY ALFRED A. KNOPF 2025

Published by Alfred A. Knopf, a division of Penguin Random House LLC, 1745 Broadway, New York, NY 10019.

Knopf, Borzoi Books, and the colophon are registered trademarks of Penguin Random House LLC.

Library of Congress Cataloging-in-Publication Data
Name: Espada, Martín, [date] author.
Title: Jailbreak of sparrows : poems / Martín Espada.
Other titles: Jailbreak of sparrows (Compilation)
Description: First edition. | New York : Alfred A. Knopf, 2025.
Identifiers: LCCN 2024008065 | ISBN 9780593537121 (hardcover) | ISBN 9780593537138 (ebook)
Subjects: LCGFT: Poetry.
Classification: LCC PS3555.S53 J35 2025 | DDC 811/.54 — dc23/eng/20240226
LC record available at https://lccn.loc.gov/2024008065

penguinrandomhouse.com | aaknopf.com

Printed in the United States of America
1st Printing

The authorized representative in the EU for product safety and compliance is Penguin Random House Ireland, Morrison Chambers, 32 Nassau Street, Dublin D02 YH68, Ireland, https://eu-contact.penguin.ie.

Dedicated to Lauren Marie Espada

CONTENTS

III. LOVE SONG OF THE DISEMBODIED HEAD IN A JAR

IV. WAKE UP, MARIO

I.

BIG BIRD DIED FOR YOUR SINS

JAILBREAK OF SPARROWS

My grandmother caught Cousin Gisela on the couch with the plastic
slipcovers that would squeak whenever anybody sat down, leafing
through the socialist newspaper called *Claridad* smuggled into the house,
worse than a wisp of marijuana smoke or a boy slipping his hands
into forbidden places. Tata's battle cry of *Ay bendito* sprayed the air.

I remember that couch, folded out so I could sleep in the living room,
before the family and the couch flew from the Bronx back to Puerto Rico.
I remember my uncle Paul, late at night, perched on the corner of the couch,
rocking like a man with a bolero ticking deep inside, tilting a bottle of beer
into his mouth, talking to me. *Do you know what that is?* he said, pointing
to the fan in the window, flapping in the heat: *Puerto Rican air-conditioning.*

Now, his daughter scanned the pages of *Claridad* for the socialistic words
colonialism and *independence, empire* and *political prisoner,* for news
of the festival where singers would sing the words a poet wrote in his cell
years ago to praise his beloved at the jailhouse door, as the crowd would sing
the verses that flew like a jailbreak of sparrows from the poet's hands.
Now, my grandmother, an informer trembling to burst with the intelligence
of a subversive plot, called her brother Roberto to say: *Gisela's reading* Claridad.

I remember my granduncle Roberto, a man blinded by his own glasses,
speeding through mountain roads and beeping his horn at every curve,
who never saw the crosses by the side of the road, who never stopped

talking as he punched the horn. Roberto sped to Tata's couch to preach
the Word of the Partido Popular Democrático and the Free Associated
State, bequeathed by the hand of Muñoz Marín, governor and friend of JFK;
the party of *Pan, Tierra, Libertad,* the silhouette of the peasant in the straw hat
on flags and buttons who would eat the *Bread,* till the *Land,* vote for *Freedom;*
the party of the jingle bouncing on the car radio, *Jalda arriba,* up the hill.
That day Roberto would not stop talking, beeping his horn at my cousin Gisela.

As he fumed the way a man fumes at a truck stalled out on a mountain road,
Roberto never spoke of La Ley de la Mordaza, the Law of the Muzzle years ago,
confiscating the ink of presses that stamped the page with the words *colonialism*
and *independence, empire* and *political prisoner,* clapping handcuffs on anyone
who sang verses that flew like a jailbreak of sparrows. The flag of Puerto Rico,
fanning a grave in the heat or asleep in a closet between the sheets, would
now become the prosecutor's proof, good for ten years in a room of stone.

My granduncle Roberto said nothing to Gisela about the 30th of October,
1950: rifles bristled like cane stalks on the plantation, clattering from hand
to hand in towns with names that fly: Jayuya, Arecibo, Naranjito, Utuado.
The rebels rose in the darkness of morning; the informers rose too, names
of subversives pinned, wings still fluttering, in page after page of FBI files.

In Utuado, the town of my grandmother's birth, the town of my father's birth,
police snipers on rooftops waited with the patience of snipers. The cloudburst
of bullets soaked rebel bodies in red, and so they turned back to sanctuary
in the last house that would open a door, firing rusty rifles from the balcony.
Then came the rumble of the convoy, the National Guard encircling them,

countless thousands of bullets splintering the wooden walls, buckling
the roof, staircase collapsing like the spine of a man thrown from the sky.

The prisoners straggled out the door, squinting into spotlights. They marched
at the bayonet's edge through town, stripped of belts and shoes, pebbles stinging
the red-striped soles of their feet, captors hooting in their ears. A machine gun
anticipated their arrival, waiting for them at the corner of a street named
for the liberator Washington and a street named for the liberator Betances.
Afterwards, a man pressed his hand into leaking entrails and looped the word
asesinos on the sidewalk, as if anyone would read it, as if a soldier would not
leave his boot print in the red letters, as if witnesses needed the word *murderers*
spelled out for them in blood, watching and listening from every window.

The next day in my grandmother's Utuado, in my father's Utuado, Thunderbolt
fighter planes flung the seeds of bombs from mountain to mountain, smoke
in the air strange as snow, interrogating the living who might testify with words
or the dead who might testify with their bodies. Soon the church in the plaza fell
silent, forgetting the chants in Latin, forgetting my grandmother's marriage
and my father's baptism, forgetting the demons in the sky. The shacks in the hills
fell silent, the men in straw hats staring at their feet, machetes only good for cane.

In towns with names that fly, Jayuya, Arecibo, Naranjito, Utuado, they lined up
against the walls, fingers woven behind their heads, bayonets sniffing their ribs,
taken by trucks to jails with names that stop the tongue: La Princesa in a land
where the princess waves from a float, Oso Blanco in a land without white bears.
The poet who knew the room of stone returned with a face of stone. The poet new
to the room of stone scribbled on stone whatever the voices bellowed in his ear.

In the year 1950, far away in Nueva York, my grandmother hovered over the steam
of rice and beans as they bubbled on the stove, swirling her cigarette in the air
to orchestrate the telling of another joke at the kitchen table. My father would soon
meet my mother, who begged him to teach her a greeting in Puerto Rican Spanish.
Tell my sister: Eres una cerda gorda, said my father. *You are a fat sow,* my mother said
to the mirror for a week, then to my father's sister in a kitchen far from Puerto Rico.
My mother would stop crying, leave the bathroom, forgive my father, marry him,
and move to Bedford Avenue in Brooklyn, where they would rush in Dodger caps
to see the ballgame whenever they heard the crowd's delirium a block away.

Years later, I heard all Tata's stories in the kitchen, a fat boy swooning over rice
and beans. I heard the saga of my father's grinning Spanish lesson till I could see
the flush of my mother's face. I heard the talk of the Brooklyn Dodgers, the Latin
chant I memorized, inherited the newspaper clippings of the World Series in 1955.

No one spoke of the ammunition belts feeding the machine gun, the men bled
like hogs for the family table, La Masacre de Utuado. No one spoke of the bombs
unthinkable as snow in a squint-blue Caribbean sky. My uncle Paul, tapping
out the beat of a bolero with his fork on a bottle, said nothing. Grandmother
Tata, who would return to Puerto Rico and spread her hands through the bars
of her balcony when she saw us in the street below, said nothing. My father, who
snarled when the Air Force called him back, the mechanic blasted by the roar
of engines till his ears crackled, said nothing. There was silence like the silence
in my father's world at the end of his life, a conspiracy of words washed away,
blood hosed off the sidewalk spelling out the word in Spanish for *murderers.*

Walking through Utuado in the year 1967, my father saw a shack abandoned
somewhere between the river and a great cave, the door's face withered

by rain and sun, the cinder block and chicken wire gate keeping no one out,
slats collapsing in the window without eyes to see. The eyes in the poster
nailed to the shack stared back at him: Governor Muñoz Marín, friend of JFK
and the FBI, the Free Associated State and the Law of the Muzzle, the *Jalda
arriba* jingle on the radio and the Thunderbolt in the sky. *Puerto Rico counts
on you,* the poster said, *to continue progress up the hill. Vote on the mountain!*
Beneath the glower and jowls of the governor, the red silhouette of the peasant
in the straw hat promised, in words orbiting his head: *Bread, Land, Freedom.*

My father cast his ballot, cradling the Nikon in his ballplayer's hands with a *click.*
At the end of his life, weeks before the VA cut a check at last to pay for the wires
that sizzled in the stereo of my father's ears, he mailed me a photograph.
On the back, he wrote *Utuado, 1967,* the words on the poster, and my name.
The poet walked through the jailhouse door. There was a jailbreak of sparrows.

MY FATHER'S PRACTICE BOOK

I saw him prowl the streets, not a cheetah in the nature documentaries he would
watch endlessly, saying *I like animals better than people,* not the first baseman
he used to be leaning at the edge of the infield dirt, but a man with a camera
in his hands, searching for the faces of the people he would call *our people*
in the circle of the lens. I trailed him, knobs of knees and elbows, first beard
curling around my jawline, camera bag on my shoulder with lenses and rolls
of film, watching him crouch and glide, waiting for the long fingers to scroll
and snap at me, my signal to stuff another roll in his hand, the whir and *click.*

I heard him boom his greeting on the street, repeating his name like a chant
to ward off calamity, *Frank Espada,* an organizer's incantation on the corner
in Brooklyn years ago, handing out leaflets about the rent strike or the picket line.
Now, he spoke the tongue of a lost island, lost mountains too big for shopping bags
to bring aboard the plane, lost names the cops would confiscate in bags as evidence.
Tape recorder on my hip, I heard the soliloquy of the witness, white shirt ghostly
in the mirror blackened by the landlord's fire, the whir and *click,* and in the circle
of my eye saw the tenants wandering the night, refugees of gasoline and smoke.

I was his son, always dubbed *el hijo de Frank,* driving my rented Chevy Impala
miles off the map to a labor camp so I could deliver the portrait of Don Pedro,
farmworker on a cane, vine of nerves crushed in his spine from too many years
stooping for tomatoes on the vine. Everybody in camp gathered to see the print,
and a man said: *Es como una pintura. It's like a painting.* Don Pedro studied

the picture of his face as if he could use it to shave, nodded and tucked it away,
sage of the labor camp, straw fedora on his head, cane squeaking across the floor.

I would drift away to an island of icicles called Wisconsin. Many years later,
my father's compañero Julio from the days of rent strikes and picket lines wrote
him a check, saying *It's time:* his first book at age seventy-six. *The Puerto Rican
Diaspora:* the faces testifying to fire or aged by labor rose up to watch him
cultivating light and darkness in every face, the veins in his hands entwined.
Waiting for the boxes from the printer, my father wrote in his Practice Book,
etching his name on the page as if learning the letters at a desk in Puerto Rico,
as if he would be graded for his penmanship by the teacher in Red Hook, Brooklyn,
who squinted at his name and said: *Francisco is too long. Your name is Frank.*

He would be signing books: first green ink, then blue, then black. He'd loop
the letter *F,* then loop it again, like faces on the subway without eyes or mouths:
he would be signing books. *Frank,* he'd write, *Frank Espada,* then *FEspada* across
the page, the birds of his name black in a white sky: he would be signing books.
En la lucha, in struggle, for Julio, with many thanks: he would be signing books.
He would practice in the Practice Book, waiting for the boxes from the printer.

After the boxes from the printer, after the luminous pages of the first book,
after the books signed and shipped to the studios of PBS or the El Puente
Academy for Peace and Justice, after the books handed out to college presidents
and poets in barrio poolrooms, after the praise in cards and letters, after the price
of the book dropped, after the boxes emptied of books, after the photographs
of sunsets taken from the deck did not sell, after the rent spilled like coffee
staining the pages of the book, after the bill for the lights glowed like a cigarette
burning a hole in the pages of the book, came the letter at Thanksgiving:

Dear Friends and Family: This is a difficult request, for obvious reasons. However,
the circumstances are, to say the least, dire, for we find it impossible to make it
on our only source of income: Social Security. At the moment, we are approaching
the edge of bankruptcy. If we cannot raise the necessary funds we will be dislocated.
The rental market is not kind to our kind, an elderly couple (82) with no solid income,
a dog and a 25-year-old car. This morning we decided we will not move from here.
We determined that doing so may just finish us off. Therefore, we are asking your
participation in this rescue operation for a loan of $500. We hope this request
does not, in any way, prejudice our friendship, which we cherish. Frank & Marilyn.

Fifteen months after the checks for the landlord and the power company,
I signed another check for my father's cremation at a mortuary by the Pacific.
He would never hear about the box labeled *Frank Espada* at the Smithsonian
American Art Museum, my fingers at the corners of a print, flipping it over
to the sight of my own scrawl in pencil on the back, the title, the date, the city.
I showed the keeper of the archives, who dangled a pair of white gloves for me.

I tuck a snapshot inside my father's Practice Book. The face in the snapshot
is the face of *el hijo de Frank,* camera bag hanging from my shoulder where any
thief on the street could snatch it away, so oblivious is that face, my glasses
crooked in the circle of the lens, lopsided smile crooked as my glasses,
my face a page without lines where anyone could write the rest of the story,
the crooked letters of his name, a book that would somehow pay the rent.

LOOK AT THIS

My father spoke. *Look at this,* he said to me. We were walking through
an alley from somewhere to somewhere else in Brooklyn. In front of us,
a man with white hair and white beard reached into a dumpster,
plucked out a bag of potato chips, stuffed his arm up to the elbow
in the bag, let it flutter to the pavement at his feet, and shuffled ahead.

Look at this, my father said again. Sometimes, he would repeat himself.
He walked up behind the white-haired man, called *Good morning, sir!,*
so the other man wheeled around to see us, shook his hand and left
a twenty-dollar bill in the handshake, all without slowing down.

We never spoke of it again. The day we left Brooklyn, he drove
away so fast he left a stack of his 78s in the closet of the apartment
in the projects. *Look at this* was all he said, and all he had to say. Look.

THE MONSTER IN THE LAKE

A city boy, I always wanted to go fishing. The DiFilippo brothers brought me
to a secret lake, where we cast our lines into the dark, the barbed lures
spinning. I snagged a monster in the lake. I fought the monster and my reel
jammed. One of the DiFilippo brothers said: *That's not a fish.* We waded
into the water and dragged a rusty box spring onshore, festooned with
the lures of failed fishermen. We plucked them off the coils and dragged it
back. Whenever we went fishing, we would have more treasures to collect.

Late that night, I felt the monster swimming beneath my feet. I walked
down to the basement and saw my father hunched over a table in his white
T-shirt and boxers. He flinched as if I caught him whispering on the phone
to a woman who was not my mother. *What are you doing?* I asked. I saw
the pages of a Spanish dictionary and a legal pad where he had copied down
the meaning of the words in longhand. *I'm learning Spanish,* he confessed.

My father the rabble-rouser with the bullhorn, my father the Puerto Rican
who spoke for other Puerto Ricans in the papers, my father who left his island
at age eleven and kissed the runway when he flew home at age thirty-eight,
my father who had the Spanish slapped from his mouth like a dangling
cigarette by teachers and coaches in the city where I grew up, could feel
his Puerto Rican tongue shriveling, coated with gravel, drained of words.

I left him alone in the basement, riddled with the hooks no one else could see.

BIG BIRD DIED FOR YOUR SINS

Barry was six-foot-six, fifteen like me, floating layups and hook shots
over our heads through the hoop in my driveway. We called him Big Bird
for dwarfing us, for his slappy feet, for the mouth that hung in a grin at all
our stories. We called him Big Bird because he would yell *foul* every time
anyone bumped him under the basket, as if we lived on Sesame Street.
I liked Big Bird and his white boy Afro. He never called me a greasy-haired
spic under the hoop in my own driveway like Frankie, the clown on the block.

On New Year's Eve, Roberto Clemente himself set foot on the prop plane
at the airport in Puerto Rico, my father's island, boxes for Nicaragua stacked
up after the earthquake, knowing the dictator's Guardia Nacional would crack
open the crates, greedy as a pillaging army, if he did not loom over them.
The DC-7, engine like a smoker's heart, four thousand pounds overweight,
sputtered a hundred feet above the trees, then spiraled into the sea on a night
when the moon deserted the sky, the keeper of a lighthouse dreaming drunk.
A crowd kept vigil on the beach. His compañero the catcher dove and dove again
between the fins that sliced the waves, till the propeller's twisted hand rose
from the sea, but never the body, never the ballplayer, never Clemente, never.

My father told me: *Roberto Clemente is dead.* I could swear my father's eyes
were red. I had never seen my father cry. This must be hay fever in winter.
My mother saw him cry once, watching the funeral of JFK on television,
the black riderless horse and the empty boots in the stirrups for the fallen.

Later, the day after the baseball writers voted Clemente into the Hall of Fame,
as the boys under the hoop toweled off and scooped up Cokes from a cooler,
I said: *When my father told me Clemente died, there were tears in his eyes.*
No one said anything, not even Frankie the clown. Big Bird stopped grinning.
Big Bird was thinking. The whine in his voice was gone when he finally said:
They only did that cuz he was Puerto Rican. They only did that cuz he was Black.

There was once an episode on *Sesame Street* where Luis and María taught
Big Bird about the meaning of death, how we all die one day, and his yellow
head drooped heavy as a sunflower. *I feel sad,* he said. I could have rolled
the numbers out like the dice in my Strat-O-Matic baseball board game:
.317 lifetime average, .414 in the 1971 Series, 3,000 hits, 12 Gold Gloves,
the only walk-off inside the park grand slam in baseball history. I could have
called on the spirit of a dead ballplayer to flood the screens in their heads
with the leap and stab of the ball against the wall in right field that saved
a no-hitter, the bark of the ball off his bat that fractured a pitcher's leg.
I said nothing. I never said anything, even when Frankie would croon his
favorite song in my face: *spicka-spooka.* The other boys would bathe in it.

The next game began. I guarded Big Bird. I stomped on his slappy feet, spiked
my elbows into his rib cage, rammed shoulder after shoulder into his back,
blocked shots by jamming the ball into his chest. I knew nothing of karate,
but kicked the air every time I yanked a rebound away. *Foul,* yelled Big Bird,
like a song on the jukebox nobody wanted to hear. *Foul.* This was my hoop,
so I couldn't foul out. I wanted to see Big Bird cry like I saw my father cry.
Big Bird sniffed; no one saw him sneeze. He squinted hard, but we all knew.

That day, Big Bird died for the sins of the fathers who cursed at the dark ballplayers on TV in the living room, where their sons could hear it all. I had a vision of Big Bird rising above the palm trees, igniting in the air like a feathery piñata too close to the spark of a cigarette, crashing into the sea, the sharks feasting on yellow feathers, Luis and María on *Sesame Street* explaining the meaning of a puppet's death as the nation mourned.

THE LIGHTS THAT BURN IN THE HOUSE OF MANY ROOMS

Valley Stream, Long Island

We wandered from room to room, lost in a house of so many rooms.
In the projects of Brooklyn, I bickered with my brother and sister
in the same bedroom, a trio of chickens squabbling over chicken feed.
In Valley Stream, I could fire a foam rubber basketball at a hoop tacked
to my own bedroom wall, the shot at the buzzer for the Knicks. In the place
we left, hands banged on the bathroom door, relentless as a zombie movie.
Here, I could straddle the toilet in three bathrooms, daydreaming of girls
I would never touch. Back in the city, my father gone at night, jailed again
for picketing or driving drunk, my mother set out the plates of fish sticks
on a table in the kitchen, edges burnt, centers frozen, and slept with her
head on the table. In the suburbs, my father would wear the apron himself,
spreading pernil on a platter in the dining room, and I would squeak my
teeth on the chicharrón, the cracked skin of the pig better than the meat.
In the Linden Projects, the Housing Authority banned dogs. In Nassau
County, a Labrador would canter through the yard, drooling on a tennis ball.

Yet, my father could not sleep. One night, like a firefighter alert to the smoke
trailing a white gown from room to room, he yelled for us to leave the house.
We gathered on the lawn as if the smoke clung to our clothes. My father flung
his arms high, a flourish of trumpets in his head, and said: *Every single light
is on.* In the house of many rooms, the lights burned in every room, a palace

on the hill, brilliant and oblivious to the villagers marching with torches.
That night, my father preached the sermon of the electric bill, all the bills
he could not pay after he paid cash for the sports car in the driveway.

We gazed at the lights in the house of many rooms: the light in the bedroom,
where I battered a lamp with the same hand Nardo held down over the flame
of a Bunsen burner to experiment with his new Puerto Rican lab partner;
the light in the bathroom, where I hid, tape unspooling in my brain, after
the hippie girl who walked with me grimaced at the bacteria on my breath;
the light in the kitchen, where my father once rose to smack me on the nose
with a rolled-up newspaper for not walking the dog before breakfast;
the light in the yard, grass paved over by a crew eager to pour cement
with the sunrise, leaving me to scrape the mounds of canine dung off
the pavement with a shovel, cursing the beast I craved in the projects.

We fled the house of many rooms, electric bills wheeling around our heads
like the pigeons my father once bred on rooftops, fleeing again as we once fled
Brooklyn, as others fled us, the only Puerto Ricans in Valley Stream. At school,
the boys in gym gave me a cake, the cursive of the baker's icing meticulously
spelling *Bon Voyage to the Spastic Spic,* then scooped it up into their faces.

Stacking boxes in the truck, a mover called Eddie bragged about his black dog
snapping his jaws at all the Blacks. My father, half deaf by that age, heard nothing.
A few years later, Mrs. Grant from Jamaica moved seven children into another
house of many rooms, her face stricken at the window, illuminated by the burning
cross on the lawn. The neighbors talked to reporters. A woman watching
on the corner said: *I don't like it. I moved from Brooklyn to get away from them.*

Twenty years later, police handcuffed a man in a lawn chair at his brother's wake
in Valley Stream, wanted for knifing his barroom friend till the lungs brimmed
with blood, wanted for torching the cross that blazed long after the light
in the many rooms of my father's house. The neighbors never told the reporters
or the cops his name: Amerigo Vespucci, named for the navigator centuries
ago, *Amerigo* scrolled across the maps of the New World, what we call América.

MY MOTHER SINGS AN ENCORE

Mothers sing to their children, and so my mother would sing to us.
Hearing a cue only she could hear, seeing a spotlight only she could see,
she would stride into the room, fan her hands in the air, and sing.

Once, late at night, I heard the screech of a creature dragged away into
the darkness by another creature. I heard the voice of my mother singing.
When my mother sings, I told my friends, *the moose come down from Canada.*
My mother sang the Mills Brothers: *You Always Hurt the One You Love.*
My mother sang the songs from *Oklahoma!, The Surrey with the Fringe
on Top* clattering down the potholed streets of Brooklyn like the junkman.
My mother sang the theme songs of TV shows: *Daniel Boone, a big man.*
My mother sang the jingle of the Mets, who lost a hundred games a year
as grounders skipped between their legs: *Step right up and greet the Mets.*
When she sang the word *hurt,* she would fold both hands over her heart.
When she sang the word *big,* she swung her arms high to show how big.

Always, she would stop the show with an announcement: *I can't sing.*

Her audience said nothing. We stared lizard-eyed at the TV or scrutinized
baseball cards as if they told the secrets of the tarot. We picked at our scabs.
Later, my mother would return, called back onstage by an unseen MC. Again,
she would sing, windmilling her arms. Again, she would confess: *I can't sing.*
We would not drop a coin into her singer's cup. We would not absolve her.

My mother hit her mark, that X of black tape on the floor of the stage, knowing that every row in the theater would rise but the first row, the only row that counted, the row roped off for family, and still she sang an encore every night.

THE BASTARD SON OF KING LEVINSKY

He was *Chicago's Fighting Hebrew,* from the Kraków family of fishmongers
on Maxwell Street, who clubbed and dazed the great Dempsey, who rammed
his head in the chest of the giant Carnera, who swung so hard he spun around,
who wore his shoes on the wrong feet in the ring, who heard the Yiddish curses
of his sister the manager leaping in the first row, who smiled for the newsreel
cameras with fewer and fewer teeth, who married a stripper, who coiled his
right hand in a fighter's pose on the cover of *The Ring* magazine, who filled
stadiums with the clamor of refugees and worshippers from synagogues.

Please don't let him hit me again, pleaded the King to the referee, squatting on
the bottom rope in the stadium where the White Sox threw the World Series,
the lights above the ring spinning two minutes into the first round, after
the hands of Joe Louis burned the grid in the brain of the King, who stumbled
facefirst to the canvas, the fighter dissolving into a fishmonger. The reporters
called him a coward, a deserter fleeing from the trenches to the firing squad.
Thirty years later, Union County College declared April 4th *King Levinsky Day,*
and a Loser's Fund of twenty dollars for a student with holes in his pockets.

When he quit the ring, the King sold ties, navy blue with a sprinkle of white
flowers, the name *King Levinsky* and a boxing ring emblazoned on the label.
He worked the tables at lunchtime in Chicago. *Do you remember when I fought
Joe Louis?,* the patter began. *Neither do I.* The King would brandish shears
to snip off a customer's tie, then pick out a new one from his suitcase.

Matches real good, he would say. He worked the crowds at the fights,
and the mobsters who always bet on the winner paid fifty bucks a tie.
When his sister died, he cried in a phone booth: *I ain't the King no more.*

I worked in the stockroom at Sears with a middleweight who could have been
the bastard son of King Levinsky. Herbie Wilens, called *The Hebrew Hitter,*
would hit me, sparring bare-knuckled to mesmerize the boys in the stockroom,
the janitor glancing up from his mail-order bride magazine. I was a boy who
drank cough syrup from the bottle, too slow to duck the right hand that
lit a match in my ear again and again, the heat spreading across my face.
Don't kill him, said the janitor. Herbie stopped hitting me and hit boxes instead,
the boom of his hands crushing the cardboard where a bicycle or lawnmower
waited for Christmas. I was a poet, so I would write a three-word poem
under every dent left by the hands of *The Hebrew Hitter: Herbie Was Here.*

Herbie would roar at the odes I inscribed to praise him on dented
cardboard boxes. We split twelve-packs of Budweiser in his basement,
though I grimaced at the foam surging in my belly. We inhaled bong hits
on his couch, though the bubbling smoke of the bong seared my throat.
I imagined my uvula, that little punching bag, bright red, the skin peeled
away, as I wailed with Jimi Hendrix singing *All Along the Watchtower.*
I told Herbie about the girl I kissed, how she hid me in her bedroom closet
till her Old Testament father shuffled to sleep, how I wrote her a poem
where she swam in a waterfall, how she dropped me and kept the poem.
Herbie told me about his father the brawler, swinging and skinning his knees
on the sidewalk. He told me about sparring the Mexican middleweight who
scorched his ribs, ranked number ten in the world. *Leo hits so hard,* he'd say.
The Hebrew Hitter trained on Budweiser and bong hits with me all night.

Later, *The Ring* would call him *inept Herbie Wilens of Gaithersburg, Maryland.*
A Puerto Rican fighter from Jersey City, who would become the champion
of the world, later a security guard grateful to Jesus, strafed Herbie with hooks
and uppercuts till he stayed on his stool, chest heaving. At the Budweiser
Washington Championship Boxing Games, signed by the matchmaker to lose,
walking to the ring in his robe with the Star of David, he remembered the right
that would spank my face till I glowed red as the light blinking on a ring post,
and Sugar Ray Leonard's older brother, *Roger the Dodger,* sprawled across
the mat. The crowd cheered the loser when he lost the split decision.

The days of sparring in the stockroom gone, the other stockboys buried
in the dumpster of my imagination, I dug for Herbie and found the body:
dead at fifty-five, cancer, the obituary listing the funeral home to visit years
after visiting hours were over, and his nickname nowhere on the record.
The Hebrew Hitter could have been the bastard son of King Levinsky,
even if he never sold me a tie in navy blue sprinkled with white flowers.
There was beer and weed on the couch, Hendrix in my blasted ear, the poem
of waterfalls where I drowned at sixteen. I carved the words *Herbie Was Here*
on every cardboard box dented by his hands, and he would roar like a fighter
on the cover of *The Ring* magazine, middleweight champion of the stockroom.

EL TIANTE SPINS LIKE A STOP SIGN IN A HURRICANE

For my twenty-first birthday I did not drink, slamming down boilermakers
at the bar, shots of Jim Beam backed with Old Milwaukee beer. I would journey
to the ballpark in Milwaukee, city rising from a sea of beer, to see the Brewers
and the Red Sox. From the grandstand, I would shout praise for Sixto Lezcano
of Arecibo, Puerto Rico, and the Milwaukee Brewers, louder than the drunks
who yelled *Hey, Six Toes* as the crowd murmured between pitches, then yelled
it again every time he snapped a throw from right field on one hop to the plate.

Baraboo handed me two tickets, grinning behind his mustache from 1884,
railroad fireman's cap over his eyes, nicknamed for the town in Wisconsin
famous as the birthplace of Ringling Brothers Circus in 1884. Baraboo played
banjo in a folk trio. At rallies, he sang a song legend says the partisans sang
to topple Mussolini from his balcony: *O bella ciao, bella ciao, bella ciao, ciao, ciao.*

Roberta was three weeks free of the asylum on the lake, where she sat for years
staring out the window with visions of sinking to the bottom. The nurses
snickered whenever she swore she used to work as a nurse on a psych ward.
She once escaped by calling a taxi. She helped me brush hospital-white paint
up and down the walls of my apartment, so I paid her with a ticket to the game.

Roberta brought a first baseman's mitt for foul balls she was certain she'd
catch like perch yanked from the lake. Baraboo pulled to the curb in his VW
van with two soccer players from Germany who had never seen an inning
of baseball. He eyed Roberta and grinned through his dangling mustache.

Roberta has a secret, he said to the Germans. She hid her face, burning
in the pocket of the first baseman's mitt. *She's a Red Sox fan,* he said. Roberta
whimpered into the mitt. I became a Red Sox fan. *Solidarity,* the song says.

I sang hosannas for Luis Tiant of La Habana, Cuba, and the Boston Red Sox.
El Tiante would spin on the mound like the stop sign I once saw spinning
in a hurricane on an island of wild ponies: saying *Stop* to the hurricane god,
wrenched by wind, saying *Stop* again. He showed his back to the batter, tilted
his head heavenward, wheeled and fired, the ball disappearing as an illusionist
would disappear rabbits at Ringling Brothers in the days of the elephants.
Maybe he saw his father in the center field bleachers, Señor Skinny, who tossed
his fadeaway for the New York Cubans, who taught his son how to grip the ball.

We saw the Brewers splinter bats and bicker with the umpire. They cursed
in the dugout at the pitcher with the shoulder blade cracked eight years ago.
Zero after zero rose on the scoreboard like balloons at the circus. Sixto lined
a single, but his teammates left him kicking the dirt at first base, a Puerto
Rican mystified by the snows of Milwaukee and the fans yelling: *Hey, Six-Toes.*

Roberta could not catch a ball hiding her face in the mitt. I prayed that Baraboo
would grab at a foul pop and topple from the grandstand the way Mussolini
toppled from the balcony when, the legend says, he heard the partisans singing
half a mile away. We filed out with the crowd, beer slapping in their bellies
like gasoline in the tank. El Tiante lit a cigar in the clubhouse after the shutout.

I never saw Baraboo and his mustache again. I would see Roberta, who won
back her nurses' license and led the other nurses singing on the picket line.
Forty years later, I would shake hands with El Tiante and ask him if he could

remember Milwaukee in August of 1978. *Four to nothing,* he said. Ringling
Brothers lost all their elephants and collapsed the big top, but El Tiante
of La Habana still fires up cigars. He tells hurricanes to stop, and the wind dies.

A DREAM OF DRUNKS OUTSMARTING ME

I was a bouncer in a bar with two doors. I stood at the front door checking IDs,
collecting dollars in a tin box for the musicians. When Billy and his catfish
face drooled over the lovers and their red wine, Billy's sister said to me:
See what he's doing? Throw him out. I listened to Billy's sister, hauling
Billy by his collar out the door. Ten minutes later, Billy drifted in the back
door, his whiskers dipping in the red wine of the lovers as he wheezed
on them. I threw Billy out again. I wanted to hook my finger in his catfish
mouth. He sprinkled piss on the curb and wheeled through the back door.

His sister said: *Billy's back.* I told the manager: *I want to lock the back door.*
The manager said nothing. He told me once that he was a helicopter door
gunner in Vietnam, high on LSD, that he remembered ten days of the war.
I was a bouncer in a bar with two doors, a dream of drunks outsmarting
me all night, circling like beer bottles on the conveyor belt at the factory.
I was always at the wrong door. I threw out the lovers and their red wine.

BETTER THAN STEALING A NECKLACE OF BULLETS

Madison, Wisconsin, 1978–79

We were living together for a week when my girlfriend said: *I'm tired of living with you.* My comrade Dog said I could stay at his commune, so I slung the duffel on my shoulder and landed on the foldout couch with the bar crucifying my body, bony as a pickerel. I ate more garbanzos than anyone else. One night, I ate half a tray of marijuana brownies, not realizing why they were so crunchy. I reeled into a room of books and read the name on every spine of every book in the room. Dog told me my nickname at the commune was *Don't Mind If I Do,* warned me they were afraid I would tear the refrigerator door off the hinges at midnight. After two weeks, they voted me out of the house and into the snow. I called my father nine hundred miles away. *Send money,* I said. *You send money,* he said. My history professor fed me lunch once a week, even though I was a dropout. He would tell the waiter: *Bring us both a bowl of sizzling rice soup, and then I will give you the rest of our order.* He always loaned me the bills in his wallet.

My car coughed like a man who used one cigarette to light another, tailpipe snapped off and sleeping in the back seat. We sputtered to the radio station. I read the news in a pledge drive baritone, learned to splice reel-to-reel tape and red-pencil the UPI feed five minutes before airtime. The engineer told me about the empty apartment between the newsroom and the transmitter for a hundred dollars a month. My salary at the station was zero dollars and zero cents. The landlady said the first month was free if I cleaned up the apartment.

A bag dripped gold under the kitchen sink, potatoes so rotten they liquefied.
The fumes made my belly spin as I scrubbed the revenge of a million French fries.
Like an archaeologist standing in the ruins, I traced with a finger the head-shaped
hole in the wall, tiptoed around the motorcycle headlight in shards on the carpet.
I stuffed a towel into the hole. I swept away the last debris of the biker brawl.
I scavenged a microwave that did not electrocute me when I plugged it in,
then stacked up cans of chili from the store on the corner. I plunged the toilet
with the curses of Ahab in my throat. They called me *The Phantom of WORT,
Back Porch Radio,* drifting into the station at midnight in my bathrobe, dropping
the needle on records at 3 AM when the all-night jazz DJ had to call his girlfriend
or study the smoke curling from the joint in his hand. My comrade Dog would
deliver free egg rolls from Tony's Chop Suey. I was awake at dawn to hear
Los Madrugadores, the Early Risers, play Mexican music for the farmworkers.

My coughing car strangled one day, rolling dead through a red light where I could
be speared from everywhere. The tow truck dumped my car in the fire lane next
to the station. Spiderwebs spread across the steering wheel. Dandelions grew
from a crack in the engine block. The fire marshal knocked on my door one day
to threaten me with a fine if I didn't move my car. *Go ahead and fine me,* I said.
I can't pay it, and there are dandelions growing from a truck in the engine block.

I was loitering on the couch in the station when the Chairman of the Party
arrived with his bodyguards. After Mao died, a delegation from the Party told
my history professor: *We've broken with Beijing.* He said: *Does Beijing know this?*
The Chairman of the Party wore his floppy cap at an angle. He wore a leather
jacket. He wore a necklace of bullets. I craved a can of chili in my kitchen.

A brown paste of beef and bean called to me. The bodyguards of the Chairman
blocked the doorway and folded their arms, wordlessly. Instead of scraping out
a can of chili, I sat in the studio with the Chairman and the host of the classical
show, who loved Mozart and hated me, since we once dated the same woman.
I could romance her in Spanish. Whenever the classical music host would ask
a question, there was a crash, as if the Chairman of the Party brought his own
cymbals to the interview. My head clanged in my headphones. The host who
loved Mozart said to the Chairman of the Party: *Sir, your necklace of bullets
keeps swinging into the microphone. Could you please remove it?* The Chairman
of the Party laid his necklace of bullets on the table next to me. I thought
about snatching the necklace of bullets and dashing out the door to pawn it
for a month's rent. I remembered the bodyguards glowering in the doorway.

The next day, there was a knock on the door. The fire marshal must be back.
At the door stood a diminutive man who collected cars. I confessed everything,
the spiderwebs spreading across the steering wheel, the dandelions growing
from the engine block, the exhaust pipe snapped off and twisted up like
a rusty Dutch pretzel in the back seat, the kind I would microwave frozen
and devour by the box. *I don't care. All I want is the body,* he said. *That's a 1968
Camaro. I'll give you two hundred dollars for it, and I'll tow it away.* The diminutive
man who collected cars towed away my car and left me two hundred-dollar bills,
two months' rent, better than sizzling rice soup, better than a can of chili, better
than the egg rolls from Tony's Chop Suey, better than stealing a necklace of bullets.

MODERATION

FOR DOG

I am the Antichrist, you cried from the window of your car as we hydroplaned
through another snow shower in Wisconsin. *I am the Antichrist,* you bragged
to the woman in the booth at the parking lot, ice in your beard, your eyes red,
and she smiled like a Lutheran waiting to wake up from a nightmare. *I am his
social worker. His medication has worn off,* I said. There was no social worker
and no medication. *I am the Antichrist,* you told your girlfriend, who rolled over.

Sometimes you were a satyr, head stuck between the curtains of the shower,
two spikes of hair soaped up like horns. Sometimes you were a wrinkled tailor,
wailing in Yiddish at the other tailor in the shop: *You're pissing down my back!*
Sometimes you were a half-wit prince, the offspring of siblings, your babble
and the clap-clap of your hands keeping the executioner busy with his ax.

All day I listened to the stream of voices from the car radio of your brain,
the dial spinning as you worked at your falafel stand, pausing only to spit
into the oil that fried the balls of mashed garbanzos, the *zap* and sizzle.

Moderation, croaked your stepfather, the dance critic for the Newark
newspaper, who would wedge a whole cake, slice by slice, into his mouth.
Moderation, you would mimic, lip jutting out, before the soliloquy on cake
your stepfather bought in bulk from the factory outlet: the box squashed

by a forklift truck, the handprint in the icing, the ash knocked off a cigarette.
Moderation, I repeated, crunching falafel in pita, even after the spit in the oil.

Your stepfather taught you the meaning of work, exiled to the meatpacking
plant in Newark, where a giant in his butcher's apron dangled you by the belt.
You made him laugh when you flailed like a boy dog-paddling. He put you down.
Everybody laughed: me, your girlfriend, your roommates naked in the hammock
at the commune, the campus lunch crowd waiting in line at the falafel stand.

After college, I heard you tried standup at the mobbed-up clubs of New Jersey.

Thirty years later, your brother called to say that, late one night, you sat down
on the porch of your ex-wife's house in cowboy boots and a ten-gallon hat,
propped a photograph of Sitting Bull up against a bottle of whiskey, pressed
a Colt .45 pearl-handled revolver to your chest, and fired a bullet caught by the fist
of your heart. You could envision her tripping across the body as you watched
one last performance from a balcony in the sky. I knew nothing of all the guns,
the syndrome, or the pills rattling like a hailstorm off the tin rooftop of your brain.

There was no social worker there that night. The medication must have worn
off, leaving a Jewish cowboy from Newark alone with his Colt .45. The night
your brother told me, I stopped sleeping. I swallow the pills in your memory.

A BUSLOAD OF SCREAMING CHILDREN

I stared at the sleep doctor staring at my chart, his domed, shaven head, his cadaverous skin, his eyes blue as the ice in an iceberg. He glanced up at me. *Stop taking it,* he said. *Now. But your office prescribed it,* I said. The icebergs in his eyes loomed closer to the prow of my face. *You will be like the others,* he said. *I see the headlines in the newspapers. You will fall asleep at the wheel and plow your car into a busload of screaming children.* He spoke as if the words were strawberries dipped in chocolate. I could almost see the red juice trickling from his mouth. *A busload of screaming children,* he said again, more to himself than to me, a man floating out to sea on an iceberg, no coat, no hat, no hair on his head, delirious in the cold.

THE CRITIC'S TONGUE DID NOT SPARKLE WITH
THE DIAMOND STICKPIN OF WIT

The critic sat at the head of the table, a whale spouting the spray of jazz history or the American novel from his blowhole, and everyone at the table leaned closer like tourists tipping the boat at a whale watch. He boomed out quotations from the masterpieces of learned men, and everyone at the table fought the urge to rise and applaud his genius grant from the foundation. His tongue sparkled with the diamond stickpin of wit from tongues gone to dust, and everyone at the table chuckled on command, nodding to each other as they jotted down the words on the cocktail napkins in their heads. He recited name after name like the announcer at the ballpark broadcasts the starting lineup, and everyone at the table salivated for the hot dogs.

I stood in the doorway, inscrutable. The critic joined me in the doorway to smoke a cigarette. He wanted to know my name, the meaning of my name, where I got my name. Espada *means* sword *in Spanish,* I said. *Puerto Rican from Brooklyn.* The critic's tongue did not sparkle with the diamond stickpin of wit: *Puerto Ricans? You've got a drug problem. Here's how you fix it. Deport the drug dealers. Deport the addicts. Deport anyone who won't talk to the police.* I told him: *We're all citizens. We can't be deported to Puerto Rico.* The critic spoke as if to instruct a man learning English: *Deport them all anyway.*

The critic sat back down, floating a word balloon from his favorite French intellectual, and everyone at the table buzzed as if they understood him.

II.

THE CITY WEARS A COAT TO BED

GUADALUPE'S FIRST-YEAR LAW SCHOOL TUMBAO

The first-year law students heard the percussion of the bench booming
all the way down the hall, around the corner, as they scurried to torts
and contracts, property and civil procedure. *Tumbao,* cried Guadalupe,
my signal to hammer the bench between my knees like a conga drum,
my hands in the L shape he taught me, the beats in each hand he taught me.
Guadalupe's hands struck the bench twice as hard, three times as fast,
swatting the wood as if to swat flies rising up from cracks in the floor
where the criminal law professor buried a body for the final exam.

We were the Puerto Ricans in the first-year class, Ray Barretto and his salsa
orchestra playing *Que viva la música* in my head like I played the eight-track
tape in my car, L of my arm out the window, hand tapping the roof. The law
students streamed around us, a few bobbing their heads in time with the beat,
others hearing the cacophony of the city that kept them awake or would blast
from cars that raced through red lights to make their hearts palpitate, still
others stuffing their ears with the cotton balls of torts, contracts, property,
civil procedure. Once, the future governor of New Hampshire smiled at us.

We were the Puerto Ricans in first-year law school. We bantered in Spanish,
drowsy in civil pro, dreading the professor's Socratic mutilation of our names,
roadkill and flies. We cursed in Spanish too, flipping through *Civil Procedure:
Cases & Problems* as the other students oscillated their hands in the air like
sixth-graders greedy for an A. We bellowed *¿Cómo está, bróder?,* the greeting

in code unbreakable at the dean's reception or meetings of student council.
We slap-boxed in the stairwell of the library, sweating through dress shirts,
the smack of hands flushing our faces red as the red of our faces in class.
The other students crept past us on the way to the stacks, a few telling us
to stop, wondering if we would ride together in the squad car or the ambulance.

Guadalupe taught me his tumbao: the beats that lived in the L of my hands,
how to spin the tumbler on the safe in my head so the combination clicked
and words in Spanish rolled like silver dollars off my tongue, the way to fold
my jacket, inside out to keep from wrinkling, a way of walking down the hall.
I was a student of torts, property, contracts, civil procedure, and tumbao.

Dominic nodded in time to the tumbao booming off the bench, always
grinning like a pumpkin gutted at Halloween, seeds scraped out of his head.
He would nod in civil procedure too, startled by his name, unable to translate
the rules of court, as if God the sixth-grader scooped out his brains. God stole
the Puerto Rican brains too. We all cursed the code we would never break.

I sat in the back of the lecture hall, small in the eye of the professor hunting us.
Today was Guadalupe's day to speak, and as he spoke my heart bounced,
a handball on a handball court. I sat behind Dom, busy in his notebook
as another student hovered over the words. I saw: *The Puerto Ricans go*
here for free. So do all the Blacks. It's affirmative action, the same as welfare.
We pay their way, work hard, and the school lets the whole jungle in the door.
Dom tossed the rumpled page from his notebook into the bin on his way out.
I unfolded the words, smoothing the wrinkles like a man ironing his shirt,
then handed it to Guadalupe, who handed it to all the hands accused of theft.

We were first-year law students. *Tumbao,* Guadalupe could have called to me,
my signal to swat the flies from Dom's head, a pumpkin left alone to crumble,
his grin crazed by the sight of all the monsters surrounding him to steal
the candy in the bowl on his stoop, to snap off chunks of his orange skull.
He denied it, so we presented the evidence, the words in his own hand.
How his face melted in a sheen of sweat, mouth drooping, wrong again.

Tumbao: the word is the child of *tumbar,* to knock down. The next day,
we drummed Guadalupe's tumbao into the bench, hands hard in the letter L,
the first letter in the word *Law.* Dom stood with us, the grin gone, listening.

THE CITY WEARS A COAT TO BED

The white army of winter spreads across the city. Boilers and radiators
die in their sleep, their skin cold to the touch in the morning. The city
wears a coat to bed. The city watches the wraith of breath rise in the kitchen.

On Friday afternoons, the judges slip off their black robes and drive home.
There is no light in the windows of the courthouse. There is no one to read
the affidavit or sign the injunction to shove into the landlord's hand so that
heat courses through the heart of the boiler and the looping hard veins
of the radiator again, no one to hear the tenant's story translated, her sons
and daughters shivering in their coats on the mattress, snot on their sleeves.

The judges and the landlord home or stopping in a bar on the way home,
she tells me instead, the lawyer who speaks Spanish and explains in Spanish
why there will be no heat this weekend, why there is no one at the courthouse
to listen, and still she pours her story into my ears till they swell to bursting.

I walk her to the doorway of the office. The secretary is in the bathroom,
the office space heater in the corner. Suddenly, I am steering the tenant
out the door with the space heater in her arms, as she says *Gracias* over
and over and I say *OK, OK,* knowing the secretary would yell my name
louder than the time a drunk with a lightning scar on his belly charged
through the door, naked but for his socks and a Salvation Army blanket.

The secretary would not miss the office space heater till Monday. I am the hero of this story, riding the bus home across the bridge, till I remember the words I should have said about the glowing coils too close to the mattress, how every week another fire rolls the smoldering wraith of winter through the bedroom as sons and daughters sleep, how every week EMTs tuck white sheets over bodies dead as a landlord's boiler. I will dream, with eyes open, of windows, the coils of space heaters and the coils of mattresses glowing in every window.

YOUR CARD IS THE KING OF RATS

We were the lawyers from Legal Aid, ready to state our case at the luncheon
of the Bar Association, the white-shoe law firms, the last of the Boston
Brahmins. I would peek in the windows of their townhouses in Louisburg
Square to glimpse the paintings on the walls, their ancestors stiff in oils.
Back at the office, refugees from the land of death squads waited for us
and apologized in Spanish, fingering eviction notices in hieroglyphics.
I looped my pre-looped tie around my neck and walked into lunch with
Jay Rose, the street lawyer I wanted to be, who bewildered landlords
like a chess grandmaster, stoic behind spectacles at the city-park games
of boyhood. We were there to ask for donations, phones, fax machines,
reams of paper, desks and chairs, to speak the tongue of *please* and *thank you.*

A man stood up to introduce me. He wore a pocket handkerchief. He spoke
the tongue of Quincy Adams the ancestor, Roosevelt the distant cousin,
grinning when he said: *I would like to introduce Mar-teen. When I say*
Mar-teen, I think Martini. That makes it easier for me to remember. I waited
for the inebriated chuckles to fade. I spoke of rats sniffing the milk on an
infant's mouth, roaches camouflaged in the Raisin Bran like raisins with legs,
ancient plumbing flooding the floors with the wrath of an ancient god.
Dessert circled the table, pastry swans gliding on plates around the white
tablecloth, an homage to their cousins on the pond at the Public Garden.
I saw the spoons dig into the crust of swans, scooping out the cherry filling.
I saw the lawyers floating away from me in a reverie of decapitated swans.

I had a law degree. I passed the bar on my first try. Now I was a magician
hired for a birthday party, boys and girls infatuated with the red innards
of dessert jiggling on their spoons. I dealt my magician's deck of cards:
Polaroids of rats in glue traps, roaches fatter and juicier than any raisin
in the cereal box, the fountain of a toilet brimming a brown soup, snapshots
we passed out to judges for injunctions to bless the landlords. How I wanted
to call out and amaze all the lawyers at lunch: *Is your card the king of rats?*
Is your card the queen of roaches? Is your card the ace of excrement? Spoons
hung in the air. I saw the muscles in their jaws grind to a stop, like the wheels
of trains pulling into the station. Some scrutinized their hand of Polaroids,
aristocrats anticipating recitation of the details at a revolutionary tribunal.
Some turned their hand face down, blackjack players praying for better cards.
Some passed, never looking at the king of rats or the queen of roaches, as if
to say: *I left no red fingerprints on the white door of those who fled that place.*

Amid the swans half-eaten, hearts open like valentines on the tablecloth,
Jay Rose, the street lawyer I wanted to be, hypnotist of landlords, stood up
before the lawyers at the luncheon and said: *We need donations, phones, fax*
machines, reams of paper, desks and chairs. Please and thank you. He got it all.

HE COULD SING, BUT HE COULDN'T FLY

We heard about the memo: Legal Aid lawyers had to ask for papers,
a green card, policing what the law called *illegal aliens,* as if they
had antennae sprouting from their heads and searching the air,
sputtering in tongues from another planet, choking on oxygen.
This would account for their coughing, not the oil tanks empty of oil.

Now, if the tenant says *I have no papers,* say, *Oh, I'm very sorry* in Spanish.
Now, if the landlord heaves the clothes out the window, jabbering about
rent like a parakeet startled by a cat, if he sneaks into the bedroom at night
and wheezes like a lovesick vampire, say, *Ay, señora, lo siento mucho,* swing
open the door of the office and point to the courthouse down the street.

When the boss would ask, *Does she have papers?,* the lawyer who lied his way
out of a date with the firing squad on a hill of skulls in Chile would smile,
creasing his unshaven face as if to say, *Here's a piñata you'll never break
with that stick.* When the boss would ask, *Does she have papers?,* I became
a wiseguy pugilist, Two-Ton Tony Galento in the movies, after the canary
who sang to the cops dropped from a rooftop: *He could sing, but he couldn't fly.*

Years before Two-Ton Tony, the brawler who trained on beer and sausage,
spoke his wiseguy wisdom on songbirds in the movies, the newspaper boys
sang of Abe Reles, Kid Twist, so called for his dexterity with an ice pick
in the ear. The night before Kid Twist would testify against Anastasia

and La Cosa Nostra, he plunged from the window of the Half Moon Hotel
in Coney Island, as half a dozen detectives played cards and saw nothing.
The headlines called him *The Canary Who Could Sing but Couldn't Fly.*

I was no Kid Twist. I knew my mother's stories of gangsters and Revelation,
informers and crucifixion in Brooklyn. I would not twist the ice pick or drop
it to sing of *illegal aliens,* skin somehow green as the invaders on the screen
of my first color TV. There was Spanish in my ear, telling me of boys in green
uniforms who juggled green mangoes with bodies beheaded at their feet.
There was testimonio in my ear, telling me of flight over mountains
and deserts to be here at last, here in the land of ice spreading across
windows like white lace curtains. They could fly, but they couldn't sing.

THE JANITOR WHO SWEPT WHERE THERE WAS NO DUST

Everybody loved the new janitor, a round man who grinned roundly all day,
who hauled away the debris of daycare in garbage bags: crushed juice boxes,
the cellophane of rice cracker snacks, napkins that wiped bawling mouths,
toilet paper that sopped up the puddles from bladders that burst like water
balloons. He swept even where there was no dust, mopped even where there
was no dirt, scrubbed the faucets silver and the bowl white even when
everybody said, *Gracias, Orlando,* and told him he could go home for the night.

We knew he was a refugee from Pinochet's Chile. We knew he was a Mormon
like my mother-in-law. I invited Orlando to dinner in Spanish. After dessert,
we sipped tea and talked in a corner about the coup. *I was in the Army,* he said.
*I was in the countryside. I saw nothing. I saw no one arrested. I saw no one
tortured. I saw no one die. Nothing?* I said. *Nothing,* he said. He wanted to talk
about the Church of Latter-Day Saints, how they baptized even the dead.

I wondered if the Church of Latter-Day Saints baptized the three thousand
dead after the coup, holy water rinsing the quicklime and mud from
the bones, raising them heavenward to sit at the banquet table with
the general and the soldiers who saw nothing. He swept where there
was no dust. He mopped where there was no dirt. We kept his secret.

TALKING TO THE HORSES IN THE DARK

Every night, on my way to the hospital, I stopped first to see them.
Boxes of gift cheese and chocolate tucked under my elbow, I walked
over to the fence, and they walked over to me: an apparition of horses,
their shuffle somnambulant, pressing their muzzles against the wire
so they could watch me, so my free hand could reach over the fence
to pat their coarse and shaggy manes. The hands that fed them oats from
buckets and brushed their coats were invisible at this hour of the night.
I never saw the patients at the mental hospital petting zoo, who would
not drain whiskey bottles in the barn, or drop a cigarette to smolder
in the hay, or flee in the dark down the road, police cars hunting them.
No one asked what they did that brought them here if they fed the horses.
No one asked what brought me here, talking to the horses in the dark.

Every night, I rubbed their noses, flashing back to Coney Island days,
the boy from the projects mounted on a diminutive horse led in circles
by a carny, bored with boys lost in imagined cowboy deeds on horseback,
collecting a dollar for the souvenir snapshot. Every night, the horses
kept their faces pressed to the wire, even after I explained visiting hours,
even after I apologized for leaving, even after I said goodbye. I crossed
the street, signed in, slung my visitor's badge around my collar, held tight
the boxes of cheddar and fudge under my arm, and with my free hand
pounded on the door of the locked ward so they heard me and let me in.

GONZO

Everybody knew Gonzo, his cigarettes and cologne, his gold crucifix,
the white T-shirt he wore to every meeting. They leaned closer to listen
whenever he spoke in the circle at the rehab center, some with eyes shut,
seeing his confessions of addiction's demons and sobriety's angels at war.

No one knew Gonzo signed his name with an *X*. The tutor at the rehab center
held up flash cards and sounded out the letters: *A, B, C*. There was no alphabet
song in Gonzo's head, no teacher at the blackboard. He said the letters, one
by one. At the letter *S,* he stopped. The tutor studied Gonzo's nose, long but
not as long as the nose of the Muppet with the same name. *S,* she said again.
Gonzo had no front teeth, no place for his tongue to go. He puffed and sprayed,
a man unable to navigate the river of his own name: *González.* He hid his face
in his hands, unlettered cards in his head, as if the tutor could not see him now.
A sob surged through him, a beast chained to the rock of his ribs for fifty years,
since the days the roosters woke him up for school in Puerto Rico. He wiped his
face clean. Gonzo was clean: clean fingernails, clean-shaven, clean white shirt.

The tutor waited, thinking: *He doesn't know his letters, but he knows every
street in Paterson by name.* She squeezed Gonzo's wrist once, then again,
till his eyes met hers. She held up the next flash card. She said: *Say T.*

BANQUO'S GHOST IN PATERSON

FOR RALPH DENNISON JR. (1989–2014)
Paterson, New Jersey

This was the first day of class in Developmental English at the community
college. Your marker squeaked across the board, jolting the students at 8 AM:
What are your hopes for this course? What are your concerns in this course?
Ralphie wrote in his notebook: *I want to major in Business Management.*
I want to open a soul food restaurant in Paterson with my sister. I am afraid
I won't finish the semester. Sometimes I make bad choices. When he handed
you the page torn from the other pages, you saw all the letters swirl in cursive,
as if from a fountain pen, the way he signed his name, the striding *R* in *Ralphie*.

One morning at 8 AM, he sat in the second row and giggled at every word,
the fumes of weed steaming from his body. The studious girl in the first row,
just here from Lebanon, twisted around to say: *Ralphie, you stink.* You told
Ralphie to leave, and so he left, apologizing as he bumped into desk after desk
on the way out. He was twenty-four, up all night, a street festival in his brain.

Ralphie found you one night in your basement office where the floor leaked,
seepage between the tiles from the bathroom next door. *I'm in trouble,* he said,
not trouble like the row of *F*s in the gradebook open on your desk, not trouble
for all the classes he missed. *I've been talking to the police and the other gang*
knows, he said. Ralphie kept repeating, like the chorus of a song bouncing in
his head till he could write it down: *I'm in trouble, I'm in trouble, I'm in trouble.*

A week later, Ralphie stopped talking. A bullet split the braids he tucked behind his ear, another informer facedown in the gravel on Rosa Parks Boulevard. His sister told the papers: *He was trying to turn over a new leaf,* but her words bled out into the gravel. The city would not keen for a man just out after eighteen months in prison for sale of drugs in a schoolyard.

No one said a word about Ralphie in Developmental English. They raised hands to ask about the chapter on sentence structure. The girl in the first row from Lebanon said at last: *This is what happens here. We have to move on.* His chair in the second row sat empty at 8 AM for the rest of the year. You saw Ralphie sitting there without a word, Banquo's ghost in Paterson, his assassin shouting: *Never shake thy gory locks at me,* his classmates hearing nothing. You saw the cursive letters no one teaches anymore, the perfect *R* in *Ralphie.*

ISABELA'S RED DRESS FLUTTERS AWAY

The other teachers warned you: *She will curse you out.* She said: *I thought you would be just another white bitch, but you're not.* You heard Isabela improvise a trumpet solo of obscenities to blast the faces of the boys circling Jorge in the hallway, the giant who would never hit back, who told everyone in your classroom to pick up their trash on the way out. Isabela sat on her desk, knees tucked under her chin, hair she snipped and dyed blond brittle as straw, bangs dangling in her eyes, mesmerized by every word from you about the play they saw on DVD, where the white boy spat in his Black servant's face. When your cell buzzed with news from your old teacher, ready to die in the surgeon's white room, she squeezed you hard on tiptoe. You were her teacher now. She was a year behind. She was about to graduate from here, the school that used to be an envelope factory until the layoffs.

Isabela flinched when she heard the door lock behind her, the smoke alarm of her mother's voice evicting a girl of smoke. She left, tattooed her mother's name on her forearm, slept on any couch she could. The school uniform that made everyone a citizen of the republic betrayed her, khakis frayed at the cuffs and dragging, the gray polo stained at the armpits. She smuggled clothes from her mother's empty house, her teacher the accomplice in the getaway car.

Her shirts and jeans swam in your washing machine, knocking on the walls of your dryer. You pulled the card from your wallet for more shirts and jeans. There was a pilgrimage to the salon in a college town where the stylist dyed Isabela's hair from yellow back to the brown of her roots, dipping her head

into the sink so she could scissor away the tangles, darkened strands dropping
wet in clumps onto the white floor. There was dinner at the college town
Chinese restaurant. She spoke of cosmetology, her own salon one day.
She was good with eyeliner and lipstick. She would text you with the word
gracias, then the word *love,* and a multitude of moon-faced teardrop emojis.

Yet, a new boyfriend meant a bed where she could sleep. He paid for a red
sateen dress to wear at graduation, the dress she wore on picture day at
school, a red flower pinned to her hair. He would wait for her in his wheelchair
as he always waited, legs withered away since the day the doctors picked
the bullet from the split trunk of his spine. One morning, as they cursed each
other, he raised a hand from his wheelchair to grab her by the hair, pulled
her close enough to kiss, and crushed her face with his fist, again, then again,
till they toppled together, crashing to the floor. His head smacked the bedpost.
She left a footprint in his blood as she staggered off. Your cell began to buzz.

You were her teacher, so you drove her to the ER. She told the nurse at intake
she slipped and fell. Your eyes met the eyes of the nurse. *You tell her or I will,*
you said. They left Isabela on a gurney in a white room and you without a chair,
so you sat on the floor, solitary witness to the slit crusting in a scab below
her eye, the purple lump of cheekbone that might be cracked, a patch of scalp.
She would comb her fingers through her hair till clumps by the handful littered
the white floor. She would sleep. The police rapped on the door to wake her,
ordered you out so they could take snapshots of the wounds under her johnny,
for the arrest that would never happen, for the charges she would never bring.

You called the principal from the hallway. *I'm fine,* you said. *You're not fine,*
she said. *You just think you're fine. This will hit you later.* There were no more

nurses, no doctor, no social worker, as if Isabela slept on a slab in the morgue
and you sat on the white floor of the underworld. Someone from the principal's
office dropped off a sack of Burger King. After school hours, when the history
teacher tapped on the door, you left. There was no bed open at the hospital.
She slept on Flaca's couch, ID tag still on her wrist, ice bag pressed to her face.

Later that night, on the college campus, poets and professors so close you
could not breathe, you would start to shake and could not stop, chilled as if
someone yanked open your collar to pour a bag of ice down the groove
in your back, an unseen fist squeezing the muscle in your chest as if to milk
the blood, your face red like the milk of the muscle palpitating in your chest,
possessed by the spirit of a dead girl not-yet-dead leaking from your eyes.
I would hold you, but could not slow the tremors, her spirit rumbling through
the tunnel of your body, the visions of hair on the floor in the white room.
Even the word *love* in your ear was useless medicine against the vertigo.

Afterwards, she saw you in the hallway and said: *Drive me to the nail salon.*
You shook your head *no.* Isabela said: *You're like the rest.* She would fade
from the hallway, a name unspoken by the principal on graduation day,
the red dress fluttering in the sky like a parade balloon escaping the parade.

At the end of the school year, somebody warned you: *She's waiting for you
at the office.* You were her teacher. Isabela wore a jean jacket, belly swollen,
pregnant by a new man. She handed you a card inviting you to the baby
shower. She handed you a single gas station rose, wrapped in cellophane.

ON FRIDAY, WE WILL WEAR BLUE

On a Friday morning twenty years ago, the new teacher saw the other
teachers dressed all in blue, blue hats, blue sneakers, looping the sidewalk
at the school, chanting in rhyme for a contract, the chant calling to her,
picket signs beckoning her. Her feet joined the other feet, weary even before
the school day began, and the teachers draped her in a blue T-shirt three
sizes too big, inscribed with the logo of the union. Cars slowed on gravel
so hands could fling cups of cold coffee, muddy grenades bursting at their feet.

The department chair watched them from the window of his office upstairs
in his goatee and ponytail, garlic steaming from his pores as if he drank
garlic tea, wore garlic cologne, lathered his ponytail in garlic shampoo.
The new teacher knocked to ask him about the eleventh-grade boys, who never
handed in papers, eyes blank as paper, lobotomized patients of adolescence.

The chair wrote poems in his goatee and ponytail, an epic gone brittle
in his desk like the half-moon of a cookie nibbled by mice, a bumper
sticker about the magic of metaphor pasted over the doorway of his office.
He swiveled to face the new teacher, and a gust of garlic wrinkled her nose.
I saw you out there on the picket line, he said. *You shouldn't be out there.*
His eye scanned the blue T-shirt three sizes too big. *As for the boys,* he said,
maybe you should wear something to flatter that cute little figure of yours.
She cursed him as the coffee bombers cursed the picket line, stalking
from the office that stank of magic, the magic of metaphor, the magic

to ward off vampires. Later, he would lurk in the back of her classroom
to evaluate her, writing his report to be sure she would never teach again.

Twenty years after the lesson of the garlic poet, at a school where the teachers
would dump him on the sidewalk like a cup of coffee garnished by a dead mouse,
she says to the other teachers: *On Friday, we will wear blue. When they ask why,
we'll tell them: We want a four percent raise.* There is blue in every closet, rhyme
in every chant. The teacher in tears at every meeting clears his throat to speak.

III.

LOVE SONG OF THE
DISEMBODIED HEAD IN A JAR

LOVE SONG OF THE MOA

I strapped my KN95 mask over my ears, ready to brave the grocery store.
Then I turned and saw myself in the grocery window, a tall and spindly
apparition with a beak. I was not man but moa, a large flightless bird
hunted to extinction, mounted in a glass case at the natural history
museum. I was ready to peck on the window with my face when
I remembered your words: *We need a pound of sliced turkey, my love.*
I wandered to the deli counter. Waiting in line for a pound of turkey,
I saw a bowl marked *BBQ Wings.* Most flightless birds have wings,
like the wings of these chickens, necks wrung so we could all have
wings dipped in blue cheese sauce for the ballgame. A farmgirl told me
that she could wring a chicken's neck while the other chickens stood
there, waiting in line, unblinking, as if to say: *What happened to Fred?*
There are no pottery shards from bowls of moa wings, since the moa
had no wings and could not even flap as other flightless birds flap,
leaving moa tracks the size of flapjacks for archaeologists to ponder.
My shoulders are wingless, so I must be a moa, hunted to extinction
centuries ago, yet picking up a pound of sliced turkey at the deli counter,
and my beak would grow pink with shame if only beaks could blush.
I tell you about the ethics of the moa, and you peck me on the beak,
saying: *But you are not a moa, my love.* This is why I am ready to bang
my face on the glass for you, screeching my love song of the moa,
a tall flightless songbird scaring the other songbirds off the branches.

LOVE SONG OF THE BAT WITH VERTIGO

Oh, your hair! How I long to stroke your hair with the tip of my wing
like the giant in that book about mice and men, so I escape your attic,
a mouse with wings, soaring above the mousetraps smeared with
peanut butter in your kitchen. You shriek at me and hand the giant
standing next to you a bat, not a bat like me, but a bat for hitting
baseballs, now a bat to hit bats, so I sail high and away, four times
around the room, a fastball slipping from the hand of the sweaty pitcher
who puts the tying run on first in the ninth inning. You toss the giant
a bucket to catch me, and suddenly I am incarcerated up against
the wall, so I beat my wings inside the bucket the way a drummer
improvises a solo, a song for you that silences the chatter in the nightclub.
The bucket dumps me into the night air, a bat with vertigo, and I flap
away upside down, searching the darkness for the light glimmering
from your hair, like the waterfall in that cave where all good bats go to die.

LOVE SONG OF THE ONE-EYED FISH

I circle the tank in the aquarium, waiting for the school groups to tumble
down the aisle like acrobats escaping the circus, clowns on their day off.
They chatter about all the sharks they want to see, the dolphins to feed.
They stop at my tank on tiptoe, fingers streaking the glass, and then
they scream at the hole in my face. I am the one-eyed fish, my eyeball
scooped out of the socket by another fish in a fight over who would hide
in the rusty cylinder at the bottom of the tank, the authentic recreation
of my environment in the bay. The teachers scream at the school groups
to stop screaming, and say to each other: *Is that all? Is this it?* We have
no sharks or dolphins here, nothing on the second floor, only a can
for donations by the door and a one-eyed fish bumping off the glass.

One morning, after I stare with my eye at the janitor mopping the floor,
waiting for the seventh grade to yell in my half-face, I see the flash of you:
an angelfish in my tank, proof that the gods of the aquarium are benevolent,
that they checked the rusty cylinder at the bottom of the tank and figured
out why the other fish was always sleeping. I am a fish in a tank, doomed
to swim in circles forever, and so I cannot hide the hole in my face. Yet,
you do not flit to the corner of the tank or dive into the rusty cylinder.
You swim with me, and we circle the tank together. The school groups
tumble down the aisle on cue, and the teacher says: *Look! An angelfish.*
If I could sing, that would be the name of my song: *Look, an Angelfish.*

LOVE SONG OF THE POLAR BEAR MASCOT AT
McCOY STADIUM IN PAWTUCKET, RHODE ISLAND

My head is stuck! I am stuck inside my head like a lunatic or a poet!

I cannot see through my unblinking eyes. This face cannot stop smiling,
as the words of my ninety-year-old mother roll around in my head:
Anyone who smiles all the time is an idiot. I listen to myself breathing,
like an obscene phone call from the days when people would say,
Hello? Hello? Who is this? in the movies. My armpits are drooling.

But they love me. They love me when I fire my cannon of plush baseballs
into the crowd. They love me when I dance on the dugout in my floppy shoes,
inches from slipping into the well of darkness. They love me when they see
my statue at the gates of the ballpark, arms stuck straight out like a crucified
polar bear in a red cap. They love me more if the team wins. They love me
more with every beer. The teenagers love me when they flick my snout to see
if I'll bite. The toddlers love me when they shriek in my face, thinking I'm real.

At the end of the game, my head is still stuck in my head. My zipper dangles,
derailed in the seventh inning, a little train skidding off the track on my belly.
I fold the chairs and tables in the ticket office, still stuffed in my polar bear
mascot costume, drenched as if I pumped my arms and legs to score
the winning run in the last of the ninth, the reverie of mascots everywhere.

I see you in the window, through the hole in my smiling mouth, and you see me, and I know you love me. You love me because you love the polar bears drifting on chunks of ice far from all the other bears. You love me because you love the polar bears who see the ice melting in a cup of beer and think of home. You love me because you love the polar bears stuck in their own heads like lunatics or poets. You love me because you love the polar bears who write poems but will never understand the train wreck of a zipper. You love me because you love the polar bears who stink, eager to nuzzle my armpit and tell me how the musk of my costume intoxicates you.

You love me, so I will be a better bear. Tomorrow, I will go to the deck with the swivel seats and find the drunk who yells at the shortstop all day, telling him to swim back to the island he came from so many times even the drunk's mother says, *Shut up, Tommy,* and fire my cannon of plush baseballs off Tommy the drunk's chest, crushing his big cup so the beer spurts into the air and showers his head like the urine of God, then rendezvous with you under my statue, where you will unscrew my head at last and I can sing this song.

LOVE SONG OF THE ATHEIST MARIONETTE

Some say God carved me from a tree, sawed off branches for my spindly
arms and painted this face on me. Some say God yanks my mouth open like
a fisherman yanks open the mouth of a fish, shuffles my feet to dance even
when there is no music, and will snip my strings the day He wants a new toy.

I say God is not my puppet master. God does not make me jump at nothing.
God does not make me rattle my fist at the empty heavens. God does not
make my mouth snap open to sing if I have no songs in my hollow head.
God does not make me love you. Forget the street preachers: God is not love.

This is love: on the night someone, not God, snipped my strings and I collapsed
in a tangle of wood, you caught me before I hit the floor. You called puppet 911.

LOVE SONG OF THE PLÁTANOS MADUROS

No, this is not a song for us, ripe plantains sliced and fried in a pan.
This is a song for you, a song in praise of your mouth and tongue,
a song anticipating your anticipation of the first bite into our yellow
hearts, a song to celebrate the delirium of the first kiss from you.

No, this is not a song for us, the alchemy of the tough skin green,
then yellow, then black. This is a song for you, a song in praise
of your nose, breathing us in, a song for your eyes as they close
to contemplate this offering, more tempting than the wafer in church.

No, this is not a song for us, flying from islands where the peasant
stain of the plátano says: *This is who I am.* This is a song for you,
a song in praise of your hands, lifting us slowly on the fork as if
to savor the delicacy of aristocrats, a song of delight in your delight.

We live to be useful, and useful we will be, warming your belly as you
crave one more. We will die heroes. We will die happy on your lips.

LOVE SONG OF FRANKENSTEIN'S INSOMNIAC MONSTER

I spend every night with my stack of DVDs, watching Karloff try to play me.
The bedroom door creaks at 2 AM, and I tiptoe, but I tiptoe like a monster,
lurching across the hardwood floor. Your eyes pop open, awake but asleep.
The bed groans with me when I roll onto the mattress, my feet splaying
off the edge, one man's ankles screwed into another man's shinbones.

Yet, you spoon me, as I drift away to the burnt windmill of dreams: the Bride
of Frankenstein, white streaks electrifying her hair, reeling around the baron's
laboratory, shrieking and hissing in my face after I whimper to her: *Friend?*
And me, *the fiend murdering half the countryside,* they say, grabbing the lever
to crumble the castle, bricks raining on our heads. Every night, I kick in my sleep,
knees bouncing in the sheets like toddlers dressed as ghosts for Halloween.
I wake up, startled by my own knees, a monster afraid of the brain sewn into
my skull, sweeping my dead convict's hand across the bed, searching for you.

You are gone. I clomp down the stairs. I see you curled asleep on the couch
and murmur: *Friend?* I stumble over another man's feet, my face looming
in close-up. You reach for me, oh bolted, screwed, sewn-up, fiendish me.

LOVE SONG OF THE DISEMBODIED HEAD IN A JAR

Like the pirates and revolutionaries of legend, heads spiked
atop the great bridge spanning the great city, I am now a head
without a body. Maybe the body ran away while I was sleeping,
slamming headless into walls and doors. Maybe my body flew
away, flapping arms, liberated until the *zap* of telephone wires.

You love me even if I am nothing but a disembodied head in a jar.
You take me everywhere, buying an extra ticket to the movies
and propping the jar on your lap so I can see the screen, hauling
me to our favorite pizza joint on the boardwalk for two slices
on a paper plate, though I can no longer chew or swallow.
You yell at anyone who stares too long at my head, rotating
slowly in a soup of formaldehyde, and defiantly smooch the jar
in their presence. We hustle dollars at the county fair. The crowds
press close to shriek when I blink at them, to gape astonished
when I sing *I'm Forever Blowing Bubbles,* the bubbles rising
from my nose and mouth, my hair swaying like seaweed.

You take care of me. You dump beard shampoo into my jar,
as if you were feeding fish. You read to me from bad novels,
and we snicker together. You leave me on your night table,
so my floating face is all you see when your alarm goes off
to wake you in the morning. *Good morning, my love,* you say.

But how can you love me? I am a disembodied head in a jar,
I cry, and my tears disappear in the soupy liquid where I live.

You are always patient when I ask. You explain, as if talking
to a Pomeranian, that you loved me when my body was so wide
I would snap wooden chairs in half by leaning back. You loved me
when my body was so lean my skin would hang like wax dripping
from a tall candle. You loved me when my body was so broad
two satchels dangled from the rack of my shoulders as I bounded up
the stairs of the train station to see you. You loved me when my body
was so spindly the sheets in the hospital mummified me as if fresh from
the sarcophagus. Now, you love me when my head swims laps all day,
and you kiss my lips pressed up against the glass with a loud smack.

Today, my head sits in a jar atop the piano in the dining room, where
the poets eating arroz con pollo at our table can toast me with their wine,
where the washing machine repairman can tell us he had a cousin
like that, where I can warble my love song of the disembodied head
for you, *I'm Forever Blowing Bubbles,* the only song I can remember,
as you play along on the piano and my head turns slowly to the music.

I MUST BE THE STEAMSHIP *MORRO CASTLE*

Every year in October, we would return to the boardwalk at Asbury Park,
sitting far from everyone, dog-walkers tripping behind dogs, shopkeepers
and their spinning racks of jellyfish T-shirts, the fortune-teller's booth
shuttered by the Madam who took the rock star's hands in her hands.
We would sit on the same bench, fingers entwined, feet propped
against the rail, to watch the churning of the tide, empty of swimmers.

Even now, my bones believe I must be the steamship *Morro Castle,* cruising
from La Habana, run aground two hundred feet from the boardwalk,
the captain in his quarters dead after dinner, no one at the wheel, no
living soul aboard, aristocrats and stowaways spun in the vortex of the sea,
lifeboats clinging to the wreck, the fire that gutted the ship still glowing.
Tourists waded up to the waist to lay their hands on the blackened hull,
and boys on the boardwalk sold postcards that soared across the continent,
the ghost ship flying from Asbury Park over the Rockies to the Pacific.

Every year in October, I testified to you the way eyewitnesses once
testified in fountain pen on postcards about the ship of dead souls
that came to rest in these waters, smoke pouring from the wounds.
You knew if a man trailed the fumes from his cigar as he waddled down
the boardwalk half a mile away, and your eyes stung at the stench,
yet you would christen this ship, smashing a champagne bottle across
the hull as they did in the newsreels of the 1930s. And we would sail.

MY BELOVED THE UNBELIEVER

My beloved is an unbeliever circumventing the multitudes of believers
on the road, the New Jersey Turnpike, the Garden State Parkway.

The believers believe, if they die in traffic, they will go to Valhalla.
Roll down the window on the highway and listen for their battle cries:
Valhalla! they clamor as they swerve from the fast lane to the exit.
Valhalla! they bellow as they tailgate, looming in the rearview mirror.
Valhalla! they rave as they fishtail without brake lights in the dark.
Valhalla! they howl as they spray the gravel of the shoulder like hail.
Valhalla! they moan as the needle on the dashboard pins to E for fifty miles.
Valhalla! they wail as they carom off the guardrails or spin around three
hundred and sixty degrees in a snowstorm at eighty miles an hour.
Valhalla! they sing at the wheel with a belly of beer, ready to raise their
goblets at the long table in paradise, toasting the gods of New Jersey.

My beloved curses the believers on the highway with the wrath
of a prophet. She knows there is no paradise. There is only the exit.

MY BELOVED THE BLASPHEMER CAUSES
A SCUFFLE AT THE BAR

Turners Falls, Massachusetts, January 2019

My beloved stands at the mike in the barroom on Third Street. The Straw
Dog Writers Guild gathers to listen. They see a schoolteacher in her
black-frame eyeglasses, in her green dress embroidered with flowers
and birds on branches, ready to gather all the children from the village
to the red schoolhouse of the imagination. Then she opens her mouth:

Now she is Cal, a man with the stump of an arm, who lost his job at the steel
mill, who lost his arm, some say, at the steel mill, who crushes a case of beer
and curses the liberals at the high school who voted to change the nickname
of the football team from the *Indians* to *Big Blue.* The boils of obscenity plague
his tongue, Christ and copulation. He is what my mother would call a blasphemer.

Two women watch from the bar, knitting and huddling over Martinis.
They clutch their balls of yarn like two cats groggy on catnip, hissing
at the blasphemies uttered by the mouth of my beloved. Calls for quiet
go unheard. One stalks out, leaving the other to stare in astonishment
at the schoolteacher channeling the voice of a one-armed, foulmouthed
ex-steelworker who used to root for the Indians every Saturday afternoon,
no spittle, no growling, no demon defying the holy water of the exorcist,
only the voice she uses to quiet the children when she says: *All eyes on me.*

The dipsomaniac's Martini tips in her hand, leaking on the bar, the olive
swirling around in the glass like an eyeball in the beaker of a mad scientist.

Disgusting! she proclaims. The president of the Straw Dog Writers Guild,
not quite five feet tall herself, approaches. *Filth!* cries the inebriate, who
spins off her barstool to slug the president of the Straw Dog Writers Guild.
My beloved the blasphemer levitates her words over the scuffle at the bar.
The Catholic school where she taught years ago fired her for writing a poem
about a broken vibrator, a violation of the morals clause in her contract,
since masturbation is a mortal sin. This is a scuffle in a bar, the accuser
not the church or the head of school, but a woman fumbling her yarn,
slamming the last of her Martini on the way out, screeching blasphemies.

My beloved the blasphemer will be heard, all eyes on her, even the olive
in the glass. The heretic preaches from the pulpit and the congregation sways.
They leave the bar eager to testify to the words levitating over the scuffle.

AWARD CEREMONY NIGHTMARE WITH
SWEDISH MEATBALLS

I was sitting at a banquet table before the awards ceremony.
A distinguished character actor, who narrated the PBS documentary
I saw last night, entered the banquet hall in a white jacket.
He was a server. I was about to ask, *Are you him?* when he fired
a Swedish meatball at my head. I could tell it was a Swedish meatball
because of the cream sauce. He fired another one and another one.
Most of them missed, but some dripped down my forehead and my neck.
I wondered why this actor kept throwing Swedish meatballs at me,
why they weren't papas rellenas, fried potato balls stuffed with ground
beef, the Puerto Rican meatball smuggled inside a crunchy potato.

I woke up cackling. My wife stared at me, as she so often does.
She wanted to know why I was laughing in my sleep. I need to be
heavily sedated. I need more pills, flying at me like Swedish meatballs.

IV.

WAKE UP, MARIO

FLORENCIA, AGAIN AND AGAIN

FOR STEVE STERN

The singers sang to Florencia Mallón today. The Threshold Singers stood
at the bedside in memory hospice and sang, as the poster of Frida Kahlo
looked on, as Florencia looked on. The only word she spoke was *No,* the only
word still left on her tongue, as she colored in her coloring book. The chorus
sang as you walked into the room, and Florencia's eyes brimmed with the sight
of you, husband, compañero. You slid behind her, arms looped around her neck,
and she leaned back, lips sprouting for a kiss on the mouth, once, then again.
Let's sing to the singers, you said. You cued up the song on your cell. You sang:

Gracias a la vida, que me ha dado tanto. Thanks to life, that has given me so much.
Florencia sang in Spanish, was Florencia again, the song drifting from a window
in the girlhood Santiago of her head. She became the writer of histories she could
no longer read, the teacher of students who would remember what she could not
remember, Florencia again. When life in the song gave her the *abecedario,*
she sang the word for *alphabet* from a spring so deep in the cavern of her brain
no neurologist could ever find it, Florencia again. When life in the song gave
her *la marcha de mis pies cansados,* she sang about *the march of my tired feet*
loud enough to startle the pack of nurses in the hallway, the march with you,
her compañero, your tired feet trying to keep up with her, the march against
the dictator in her Chile, all the songs the crowd would sing, Florencia again.

How do you kill an idea? Florencia said to me when I asked why so many had
to die in Chile, at an age when I still had to ask, six words I will carry like tiny
shells from Chile as long as I remember what I remember, Florencia again.

Gracias, you sang with Florencia at the bedside to the singers at memory
hospice. You handed them the sheets with the printed lyrics of the song.
Next time, when you come, you can sing it to her, you said, Florencia again.

My teacher, tomorrow you will turn the knob all hands dread as if the steel
would liquefy their fingers, walk through the door once more and sing,
and so Florencia will become Florencia again, Florencia again and again.

INSULT

FOR WILLIAM CARLOS WILLIAMS (1883–1963)

Stroke: insult to the brain, leaking blood; insult to the right eye, now blind;
insult to the right hand, now dead; insult of the X-rays, lighting up the skull
like a bulb; insult of doctors telling him what he already knew, the poet-doctor
who brought three thousand infants to light by the river and the silk mills
of Paterson; insult of the black bag open and empty after the last house call;
insult of the bills clogging up the mailbox, sliding off the kitchen table.

The report of *Loyalty Data* in his FBI file had its own beats, words like
the stutter of tommy guns in the G-man movies of Hoover's imagination:
Chairman of the Local Committee for Medical Help to Loyalist Spain,
State Committee of the New Jersey Civil Liberties Union, American
Committee for Protection of Foreign Born, Free Speech Rally Wednesday
at Carnegie Hall for the Hollywood Ten, New Masses, Partisan Review.
A friend told the G-men: *His charitable nature would explain his membership*
in doubtful organizations. The radio demagogue railed about the poet
who jumped on the I Love Russia Trolley and stayed aboard for the ride.
The G-men interrogated the chief of police, the editor of the newspaper
in his hometown, his neighbors on Ridge Road. The appointment as
Consultant in Poetry to the Library of Congress melted away, delay after
delay, the poet waiting for word as if lost again in the labyrinth of hospitals.

May 1953: The poet glanced at the white sheet in the typewriter, the blank
calendar on the wall, nowhere but ice to plant his feet, nowhere but ice to fall.
He struck the keys left-handed, one finger at a time, cursing all the typos
and the strikethroughs, not for a poem but a gig, tapping out the signals at sea
to Swarthmore College. *To whome it may concern: Since hearing from the man*
charged with securing XXXX speakers for coming events, I have mislaid his name
and don't XX know how to establish communication with him. There is I am
told a Professor Hoffman on your English faculty who might be able to help me.
I would appreXciate, other means failing, being put in contact with him. Thank you.
He left the letter *e* at the end of *whom;* he could not turn that wanderer away.
At the foot of the postcard, he carved his name in poet's ink left-handed,
the tall *W* in William, the hunchbacked *C* in Carlos, the shaky *W* in Williams,
one man speaking poems, one man walking on a cane, one man sitting down.

Two years later, from his insulted brain would swim the words: *It is difficult /*
to get the news from poems / yet men die miserably every day / for lack / of what
is found there. The doctor knew about the strokes to come, that his brain would
one day stop speaking to his body, like furious lovers sleepless back-to-back.
The poet knew about the wrong hand rapping the keys, one eye burning all night,
the typos, the strikethroughs, the curses, the gig, the poem, the poem, the poem.

THE FIREFLIES OF BELMONT AVENUE

FOR JULES CHAMETZKY (1928–2021)

I see you as a boy, ten years old, at your father's butcher shop on Belmont Avenue
in Brooklyn, the words *Kosher Meat* spelled out in Hebrew across the window,
the chickens dangling in the window, the words unbroken, the glass unbroken,
the butcher unbroken. I see you watch your father as we watch our fathers,
scanning the Yiddish newspaper at the counter, Lucky Strike glowing in his mouth,
as you wait for his words to rise and fall like fireflies or embers, learning how
words fly or burn, when to cup your hands to catch a word, when to jump away.
The customers would lean across the counter to buy chickens from your mother.

I see you at eighty. I watch you as we watch our fathers, as I would watch my father
and his cigarette, the organizer who could rouse the crowd, waiting for his words to fly
or burn. I am a boy from the old neighborhood in Brooklyn, and you are the teacher,
slicing up Hemingway like a chicken boned across the page. Yet, for me, a poet without
the first strand of gray in his beard, your words are always fireflies. I would cup them
in my hands, and see them glow, as I see them now, even as I lift my hands to let them go.

MY DEBS, MY EUGENE

FOR EUGENE POVIRK (1948–2022) AND SOUTHPAW BOOKS

Your father, the union man, named you for Eugene V. Debs, the saint of socialism.
When Debs spoke, everybody wept. When he spoke against the Great War,
the judge sentenced him to ten years, and the gaunt man in tweed rose to say
at the hearing: *While there is a lower class, I am in it, and while there is a criminal
element, I am of it, and while there is a soul in prison, I am not free.* At the rallies,
they wore red buttons with his face and the words: *For President Convict No. 9653.*
A million voted for him as he sat in jail. On the day he left, the convicts streamed
into the yard, mobbed the gates of the penitentiary, and cheered for him
when he waved goodbye. Fifty thousand people swarmed for a sight of him
at the train station. Brass bands played a fanfare. The crowd hauled Debs
away on their shoulders like a hero of the gridiron or the boxing ring.

There were no brass bands when you said the word *No* to refuse the draft
for the war in Vietnam. There were no buttons with your face when LBJ
indicted you. The crowds did not overflow the sidewalk when you painted
a house or hammered the roof. You were never the saint of socialism.

Yet, I made my pilgrimage to see you, a sage in the mountains, cloistered
in his cave of books, the words of Eugene V. Debs on a sign nailed up over
the doorway in your shop. Waving a flashlight, I would squeeze into the stacks,
bookshelf after bookshelf of dead rabble-rousers and hell-raisers, strikers

and muckrakers, poets and socialists, words stirring in the darkness
when I stirred up the pages, intoxicated by the scent of ink and paper.

When I stumbled at last back into the lit world, books spilling in my arms,
you knew them all by name, translated the ancient script carved by hand
on the page, told me who shot the poet in a flophouse, who refused to testify
and slept sleepless in jail, who led the strikers in the singing, who died of drink
to leave the books she loved in her husband's chilly mansion, all the orators
on street corners who mesmerized thousands and now mesmerized no one.

I saw your hands that could build a house pick up a brush to dab wheat paste
on the cracks of a page fallen from a book, and the flying devils dashed off
on the page by the hand of the artist flitted to life again, and the artist
charged with sedition woke up at his trial, drowsily listening to his lawyer.

One day, my hands would open a book with brown spots of age on the leaves,
fingertips tracing the inscription inked to a poet now forgotten: *For my young
and loyal comrade, with very much love, Eugene V. Debs, March 30th, 1916.*
I saw the face on the button: Convict No. 9653 for President. He was sitting
in your shop, piles of books somehow not toppling on his head. He was reading.

You were my Debs. You were my Eugene. There should be a button with your face,
so today I wear the button with your face. There should be a crowd to meet you
at the train station, so today I am your crowd. There should be brass bands
for you, so today I am your brass band. There should be a penitentiary
of convicts cheering for you at the gate, so today I cheer as you wave goodbye.

THE PUERTO RICAN WITH THE BOLSHEVIK NAME

FOR VLADIMIR MORALES (1951–2022)

He shook my hand and said: *Vote for me.* I knew him only from the lawn signs
everywhere, the Puerto Rican with the Bolshevik name running for School
Committee. The last time, I didn't vote for him. I was too busy bellowing
my poems in Winston-Salem, North Carolina, the land of cigarettes,
where somebody said: *Are you a communist?* This time, I voted for him.
One day, he shook my hand and said: *Help me raise the Puerto Rican flag
on the Town Common.* I didn't help him raise the flag. I was too busy bellowing
my poems in Newcastle, England, the land of coals, when a white-haired
gentleman raised his hand and said: *I'm sorry, sir, but where is Porto Rico?*

E. Montgomery Reily knew. Harding's man, the island governor called *King Monty,*
who never had to shake hands with a Puerto Rican and say *vote for me,* said:
As long as Old Glory waves over the United States, it will wave over Porto Rico.
The only flag to raise is the flag confiscated by King Monty's chief of police.
The only flag is the flag of rebels caged like mice for experiments in electricity.

In another century, another country, we raised the flag on the Town Common.
Sometimes we struggled in the clatter of dead leaves, wrestling with the flag
as it flapped up and down the pole, the editor of the neighborhood Puerto
Rican paper aiming his camera at us to blur the poet and the politician.
Once the rains came, and I gave directions from the black wing of an umbrella,

as the Puerto Rican with the Bolshevik name hoisted the flag like a kite into the raindrops. *Looks great,* I said. We scurried off for breakfast burritos.

The raising of the flag, the flurry of petitions, the tally of votes at Town Meeting, the rallies on the Common, the resolution against the Navy war games cratering the coral reef in Vieques, all dissolved away the day the Puerto Rican with the Bolshevik name slid behind the wheel and drove me to the Emergency Room, my hands gripping my belly, the morphine IV and the surgeon's knife waiting for me as he waited for me in the room with the TV stuck on Fox News and the snack machine guzzling quarters. Now, too late, I sign my name to his petition. I am not too busy anymore.

THE LAST WORDS OF HURRICANE HI

FOR HIRAM BITHORN (1916–1951)

I am a member of a communist cell on an important mission. The cop
in El Mante who shot him in the belly heard the gut-shot ballplayer say it.
I am a member of a communist cell on an important mission. The doctor
who drove him to the hospital in a city two hours away heard him say it.
I am a member of a communist cell on an important mission. The editor
of the town newspaper, said the headlines the next day, heard him say it.
I am a member of a communist cell on an important mission, the trio sang
like a ballad on the radio, the last words of the first Puerto Rican in the majors.

Daydreaming of a comeback, he drove through México, pitching arm slung
across the wheel of a 1947 Buick. The cop stared hard at his papers. After
a hose sprayed the blood into the gutter, the chief of police steered his new
Buick through El Mante on whitewall tires, the crooning of a trio on the radio.

The bullet in the pitcher's belly knew nothing of the first Puerto Rican
in the majors, his baseball card, his eighteen wins or his seven shutouts
for the Cubs in 1943. The bullet in the belly knew nothing of his windup
or the ball he fired into the dugout to scatter the other team after the jeering.
The bullet knew nothing of the pitcher's nickname in Chicago: *Hurricane Hi.*

The judge saw the ceiling fans wipe away the last words the pitcher never said, and the zero of the cop's mouth when he heard the sentence read: *Eight years in jail for the bullet in the belly of the pitcher.* Shovels uprooted Hurricane Hi from a common grave to ship him home, all arms and legs, pockets full of dirt.

The first Puerto Rican in the majors would trade the tall letters of his name, greeting the fans at the stadium in San Juan, for a ride in his 1947 Buick. The hero of the island would trade his windup cast in bronze for a Buick with whitewall tires. Hurricane Hi would trade his nickname, his baseball card, the seven shutouts that led the league, the zeros of every bigot's mouth after they scattered in the dugout, for his Buick with the whitewall tires racing far from El Mante, the fireworks of New Year's Eve beckoning in the windshield.

OFFICER MARK DIAL, WHO SHOT EDDIE IRIZARRY, WILL BE FIRED FOR INSUBORDINATION

— headline in The Philadelphia Inquirer, *August 23, 2023*

The white balloons rise in the 100 block of East Willard Street.
Some of the white balloons float the word *Justicia* into the sky.

The officers in the white cruiser saw Eddie hop the curb and would send
a bouquet of words into the sky above the 100 block of East Willard Street,
bumping each other as they spiraled through the clouds: *driving erratically,*
they said, *lunged with a knife,* they said, *multiple commands* and *shots fired.*
At the ER, doctors bathed Eddie in white light to pronounce him dead.

Eddie's aunt Zoraida knew her Eddie, the reggaetón in his headphones,
the wheelies on dirt bikes, the cars that would roar back to life whenever
he dipped his oil-black hands into their entrails, the pocketknife to strip wires.
She remembered the boy from Ponce, Puerto Rico, cowled like a monk
in his black hoodie, never a jail cell, never a ticket, never a word in English.
Zoraida and the cousins canvassed the 100 block of East Willard Street,
pushing doorbells, searching for a doorbell video, watching it on a loop:

Eddie is parallel parking, careful not to squash the orange cone under the tire.
The cruiser glides alongside, no siren, no lights. Officer Dial shouts *Hands*
in the air and *Drop the knife* in the language of detours Eddie could never read,

circles like a skater on the ice of August around Eddie's car, popping six shots,
shattering the ice of the window rolled up on the driver's side, cracking the ice
of the windshield. The horn bleats, a goat terrified of the sacrificial knife,
and Dial yells to stop the horn, as if Eddie's soul is stuck in the traffic to heaven.
The cops drag him out by two arms and a leg, and the horn's heart stops beating.
They dig in the seat for the three-inch pocketknife he pressed against his knee.

The police chief in her white uniform announces that Officer Mark Dial,
who shot Eddie Irizarry, will be fired for insubordination, now that he
is silent as the horn in Eddie's car, now that he is silent as Eddie. The words
jail and *murder* do not drift from her mouth to tap the ceiling at the press
conference. The department will backtrack to investigate the lunging
tongue, how the fable of the knife slipped from their throats into the air.

Eddie's coffin is gray, rising on the shoulders of pallbearers in white T-shirts
that say *Justice for Junito,* like Junior, Eddie the father left to gaze at the black
hands he would bequeath to his son, who learned from him all the spells
to spark the hearts of engines, the smoke fading away like ice in August.

The newspaper reports that *ABC's Next Bachelor is a Tennis Instructor
from Montgomery County.* At the vigil in the 100 block of East Willard Street,
the white balloons rise. Some balloons float the word *Justicia* into the sky.

WAKE UP, MARIO

FOR MARIO GONZÁLEZ ARENALES (1994–2021)

He's not doing anything wrong. He's just scaring my wife.
    — call to the Alameda Police Department, April 19, 2021

They watched him from the window of the house, a man at the fence
in a crooked wool cap, chipping at their tree with a comb, liquor bottles
in a shopping basket by his feet. They heard him speak to the wife's
mother in the yard, tongue thick in his mouth, heavy with lamentation.
He could be the Aztec god of pestilence, no mask, breathing the plague
on them through walls and doors. The Mexican nanny might be able
to read the hieroglyphics tumbling from his mouth, but she was wheeling
a stroller through the streets of Alameda, the trees bowing deeply.

On the news, the bodycam clip wobbles like the video at a barbecue.
The cops are cheerful as they encircle him in the park across the street.
He says his name is Mario. One cop scolds this refugee from Oakland about
drinking in our parks, wants ID so they can be *on our merry way.* Mario says:
Merry-go-round? He steps up on a tree stump as if to ride it. The cops climb off
the spinning horses of Mario's imagination, tugging at his arms as he peeks
at them from under the cap. Now they are cowboys at the rodeo, but Mario is not
a steer, crashing to the applause of hands that would carve him into steaks.

The cops shove him to the ground, facedown. Mario squirms and bucks;
he is the prize at the county fair, a beast who tries to calm his captors,

so he spits all the words he knows to make them stop: *Oh God, please,*
thank you, and *sorry, I'm sorry, I'm so sorry. I forgive you,* says one cop,
as the other cop digs his knee into Mario's back, where it stays even after
they cuff him, even after the first cop says: *Think we can roll him on his side?*
He asks Mario for his birthday, as if there will be a barbecue in the backyard
at the cop's house, and Mario, facedown in the wood chips and the dirt,
with the other cop's knee pressing into his back, wheezes the year: *1994.*

There were cries, then silence. There were no last words. In medieval days,
the prisoner at the block would forgive the headsman and drop a coin into
his hand for a clean strike of the blade. In Salem's Puritan days, a man accused
of witchcraft, after two days of stones stacked on him, sneered: *More weight.*

There were no last words from Mario when they rolled him over at last.
The last words were in the headlines that same day, jury deliberations
two thousand miles away in Minneapolis, the case of a cop kneeling
on the neck of a Black man, facedown and handcuffed, for nine minutes.

In Alameda, the cops began CPR and their incantation over the asphyxiated body:
Wake up, Mario, wake up, as if he would be late for school on class picture day,
as if he would miss his shift at the pizzeria where the paychecks dwindled away,
as if he had an autistic brother waiting at home for Mario to help him step from
the shower, button his shirt, comb his hair. His autistic brother still waits for Mario.

The man who called the cops, his wife's hand gripping his shoulder,
says *We greatly regret what happened and never intended,* says *Terrible*
things are being said about us, says *Our autistic child is able to read*
and is terribly sensitive. The sign in front of the dark house says: *For Sale.*

The merry-go-round in Mario's imagination grinds on, creaking
day after day: the caller who presses the button to make the horses go,
the cops charging like cavalry after the renegade, the dead man galloping
ahead, escape impossible, his horse impaled on a pole, kicking the air.

The Mexican nanny called Crucita blames herself for rolling the stroller back
too late. She visits the altar for Mario across the street from the tree missing
a sliver of bark from his comb. The roses wreathing his face shrivel to plastic,
balloons gone flat, votive candles cold. There is an autopsy after the autopsy.
The coroner keeps the city's secrets, a priest hiding in the confessional.

In her sleep, Crucita sees Mario, sometimes a body splayed across the street,
breath squeezed from his lungs like the last note from the pipes of a calliope,
sometimes breaking free, the painted horse lunging away, as he rides
along the coast to the deserts of Baja California, down mountain trails
off the maps of Yanqui generals and their armies, deep into the songs about
bandidos too clever to be caught, revolutionaries the bullets cannot kill.

THE FACES WE ENVISION IN THE SCRAPBOOK OF THE DEAD

FOR CAMILO PÉREZ-BUSTILLO AND THE CITY OF EL PASO

A freak fall, you said. *A bad landing,* you said, a Colombian from Queens
always wandering a map of unknown places. The tumble down the stairs
of the brownstone in Brooklyn ripped your knees from their moorings,
ruptured both quadriceps, and in the whirlwind of an instant you could see
the flash between walking and not walking, breathing and not breathing,
like a fighter wheeled away from the ring on a stretcher as everybody prays.

The surgeons resplendent in white, priests hearing the god of ripped bodies
speak to them, screwed your knees back on, sat you in a wheelchair the way
a ventriloquist props up the dummy on his knee, and sent you home. In El Paso,
blood seeping through the bandages, the bathroom a soccer field away,
you waited for the boy you named Centli to lift you up, his arms suddenly
thick, your head suddenly on his shoulder. You called all your compañeros
the night he was born, jolting them from sleep, translating the Nahuatl name,
tender grain, deity of maíz in México. Now, he drove for Lyft, steering
inebriated soldiers from Fort Bliss to the strip clubs, who fisted dollar bills
for him, then the garters of the girls. Your girl, Lucecita, crossed the bridge
from Juárez, a waitress swerving from table to table at the diner, her mother's
name on the badge of her uniform. For you, she scrambled eggs with green chiles.

The day came you saw in sleep, day of muscle gripping bone like vines curling
around the wrinkled trunks of trees, day you could walk with a cane in each hand.

At the Walmart by Cielo Vista, near the movie house where you would see
Centli's Marvel heroes and their ropes of muscle, you picked out your canes
with ceremony, your boy and girl as witnesses, scrutinizing the aluminum bones,
the gray rubber handles, suction cups anchored to the floor, those diminutive
spaceships. You paid for the tools of liberation and a roast chicken at the checkout
counter. No one could envision all the faces in the scrapbook of the dead.

You would stand with the solitary man from Brooklyn and his sign that said
Free Them at the migrant adolescent internment camp in the desert of El Paso,
and found your lawyer's tongue as a carpenter finds the hammer, words nailed
in the air, then evaporating in the heat for reporters who could never write as fast
as you could talk, who said, *Could you repeat that?* till the delegations from
Congress swept into the desert with calls to investigate. You would stand
at the microphone, thin as the mike stand, to tell the rallies on the border
about the militia patrolling the desert in camouflage, the men who raged
of *invasion* to the migrants shivering in the sand at gunpoint, so you kept
talking, like a man at gunpoint, till the vigilantes evaporated in the heat.

August 3rd, 2019: at the table with Centli and Lucecita in la Ciudad de México,
you saw again the flash between walking and not walking, breathing and not
breathing in the headlines from El Paso. The shooter left his job selling
popcorn at a movie house to navigate six hundred fifty miles across the map
of Texas, stopping only to scald his throat with coffee or stare in the mirrors
of gas station bathrooms, the manifesto he nailed to the message board
shimmering in the mine shaft of his head: *The Hispanic invasion of Texas,*
open borders, free health care for illegals, cultural and ethnic replacement.
He meandered through the aisles of your Walmart by Cielo Vista, another

boy who would drizzle extra butter on the popcorn, then came back
wearing headphones and safety glasses, like a mantis with eyes swiveling
in search of prey, the AK-47 at his shoulder, the Mexicans in his sights.

Later, as the scrapbook of the dead flipped across screens and newspapers,
you saw a face you knew, a man oblivious to the headlines and captions
creeping at the edges of his snapshot like black bunting. Arturo drove a bus
for the city of El Paso, marched for the Army and the Chicano Movement,
sat a few times at the back of your class called Human Rights on the Border
and would raise his hand. How you long for a beer in a bar with him now.
How you wonder if your lawyer's fireworks show of words burst in the sky
of the boy with the rifle, why he drew a circle on the map around El Paso.

In the hallucination you cannot swat from your eyes, you lean on your canes
at the Walmart, close to the checkout counter where the bus driver bags
the last of his groceries, as the crowd stampedes to the back of the store
with the gunshots popping in the parking lot, and your knees tell you
what your thudding heart already knows, that you cannot flee to dive
and roll under a table or a storage bin. Centli and Lucecita stand with you,
refusing to run with the others, leaving their father wobbly on his canes
in the medical supply aisle to face the bullets alone. Your boy's arms
are suddenly thick around you. Your head is suddenly on his shoulder.

THE SNAKE

At the Save America rallies, after the damnation of the *criminal aliens breaking across our borders* and *1,900 percent more murders,* he would ask the crowds if he could read a poem. *This has to do with immigration,* he'd say. The crowds would whoop and yip. He'd read *The Snake,* words stolen from a song, from the hand of a dead Black singer who could not snatch it back, a jazz fable spun on vinyl, spun first by the fabulist of Greece centuries before Christ.

The crowds would listen to the poem: Bikers for Trump, Cops for Trump, Uncle Sam in his beard, the Statue of Liberty in her crown, the millionaire who sells pillows on TV. They would testify in T-shirts that said, *Jesus Is My Savior, Trump Is My President.* They would hoist the Stars and Bars or signs that rhymed, *Trump 24 or Before.* They would see the movie of the poem in their heads:

The snake frozen on the road, the woman scooping him up tight to nurse him with milk and honey by the fire, the incandescence of his skin brought back to life, the woman's kiss and the viper's venomous bite, her question *Why,* then the words oozing from his tongue: *You knew damn well I was a snake before you took me in.* The crowd would howl at the moral, at the punch line, at the *tender woman* who would die of tenderness. Like a preacher spelling out the lesson of a parable, their president would repeat: *Immigration.*

As they slept — the bikers and the cops, Uncle Sam and the Statue of Liberty, the millionaire on his magic pillow — adolescents from Guatemala scalded the killing floors at the slaughterhouse in Grand Island, Nebraska, their hoses like snakes spewing rivers that bubbled in the steam. Around them, the blades of skull splitters and bone saws waited for their fingers to slip, fangs lurking in the murk of early morning, in the daze behind the goggles on the faces of adolescents from Guatemala, sleeping the next day at Walnut Middle School, shaken awake by teachers who spotted the acid burns on their hands.

BREVE PAUSA

FOR JUAN ANTONIO CORRETJER AND CONSUELO LEE TAPIA

In the photograph, the poet leans over to kiss his wife. He wears a black
suit and a black tie, as if there will be a ceremony and a medallion hung
around his neck. His hair is white and crowns the back of his head. Her hair
is white in waves. She lifts her face to kiss him through his white mustache.

This is a despedida. They are kissing goodbye. The charge is conspiracy again.
The officers born years after his first incarceration lead him away to Castillo
de Ponce. The officers lead her away to the women's prison at Vega Alta.

The evidence is in the poetry. As the convoy of the empire's army rumbles in
the dark, past the mountain town where one day they will be buried side by side,
the poet says to his beloved: *Esta es pausa / para el amor. Es sólo / breve pausa.*
The poet watches her sleep. *This is a pause / for love. It's only / a brief pause.*

THE IGUANAS SKITTER THROUGH THE CEMETERY BY THE SEA

Viejo San Juan, Puerto Rico

The iguanas slither from the branches of trees splintered by the hurricanes.
The iguanas crawl from the cracks in the ground split by the earthquakes.
The iguanas rise from brown floodwaters that carry bridges to their doom.
The iguanas multiply through the night of blackouts in hospitals and morgues.
The iguanas burrow beneath roads to bury their eggs in the lungs of cities.
The iguanas slap their clawed feet as they churn the earth of the farmer's field.
Iguanas rip the rough skin of mango; iguanas rip banana; iguanas rip papaya.

The iguanas skitter through the cemetery by the sea, tails snapping when
they disappear between the crosses, sunning themselves on the walls,
hiding in the crevices of crypts where families still cling to each other
beneath the weathered stone. The iguanas stare stupefied at the bust
of a mustachioed poet who died after the bacteria feasted on his heart.
The iguanas know nothing of José de Diego, his songs of the guaraguao
and the pitirre, the hawk fleeing from the two-ounce kingbird, the slash
of claws to save her young still blind in the nest. The poet's hawk is *long
and dark with imperial wings,* the poet's kingbird *an arrow through the neck.*

An iguana warms his belly on the flat stone that says: *Pedro Albizu Campos.*
The iguanas know nothing of Albizu: the lawyer and the cane cutters' strike,

the crowd listening in the rain, cane stalks in their heads igniting like torches.
The iguanas learn nothing from El Maestro, his staccato tongue on the radio
splitting the ground under the boots of the military governor, collapsing
the courthouses and flagpole of empire. The iguanas keep vigil at the tomb,
burial stone white as the stone of *seditious conspiracy* that buried him, stone face
of thirty years' incarceration, subversive tongue gone to stone after the stroke.
The iguanas forget the thousands in black sweeping his coffin to the edge of the sea.

The green of the iguanas in the cemetery is the green of soldiers in uniform.
The green of the iguanas in the cemetery is the green of felt at the casinos.
The green of the iguanas in the cemetery is the green of cash on cruise ships.
The green of the iguanas in the cemetery is the green stacked in steel vaults.
The green of the iguanas in the cemetery is the green of lawn after lawn hidden
by gates, the green of mangoes in a bowl on every table of the absentee landlords.

In the movies on the drive-in screens and Saturday matinees of the Cold War,
iguanas played the dinosaurs, horns glued to their snouts, frills pasted to their
heads, thrashing in close-up struggle with other iguanas over *The Lost World.*
The dead eyes of the iguanas, keeping vigil over the city of the dead, will never
see the asteroid of their extinction, the earth melting to suck their bones into
whirlpools of mud, the wave sweeping them to sea, the flight of the poet's kingbird.

ACKNOWLEDGMENTS

These poems have been published or are forthcoming in the following publications:

The Arkansas International: "Love Song of the Atheist Marionette," "The Critic's Tongue Did Not Sparkle with the Diamond Stickpin of Wit"

Arriving at a Shoreline (Great Weather for Media): "Wake Up, Mario"

The Bombay Literary Magazine: "Officer Mark Dial, Who Shot Eddie Irizarry, Will Be Fired for Insubordination," "Guadalupe's First-Year Law School Tumbao," "My Mother Sings an Encore," "Love Song of Frankenstein's Insomniac Monster"

Fatal Force: Poetic Justice (Moonstone): "Officer Mark Dial, Who Shot Eddie Irizarry, Will Be Fired for Insubordination"

First of the Month: "Big Bird Died for Your Sins"

Freeman's: Animals (Grove Atlantic): "Love Song of the Moa"

Kenyon Review: "Florencia, Again and Again," "My Beloved the Blasphemer Causes a Scuffle at the Bar"

Labor: Studies in Working-Class History: "A Dream of Drunks Outsmarting Me"

Madison Magazine: "Better Than Stealing a Necklace of Bullets"

The Massachusetts Review: "The Fireflies of Belmont Avenue," "The Janitor Who Swept Where There Was No Dust"

Michigan Quarterly Review: "My Father's Practice Book," "Insult"

Morning Star: "He Could Sing, but He Couldn't Fly"

The Nation: "The City Wears a Coat to Bed"

The New Yorker: "Your Card Is the King of Rats," "Gonzo"

North American Review: "The Faces We Envision in the Scrapbook of the Dead," "Jailbreak of Sparrows," "My Debs, My Eugene," "Talking to the Horses in the Dark," "Love Song of the Polar Bear Mascot at McCoy Stadium in Pawtucket, Rhode Island," "The Last Words of Hurricane Hi," "El Tiante Spins Like a Stop Sign in a Hurricane," "Officer Mark Dial, Who Shot Eddie Irizarry, Will Be Fired for Insubordination," "Guadalupe's First-Year Law School Tumbao," "My Mother Sings an Encore," "Love Song of Frankenstein's Insomniac Monster"

Paterson Literary Review: "Love Song of the One-Eyed Fish," "My Beloved the Unbeliever," "Moderation"

Pensive: A Global Journal of Spirituality and the Arts: "On Friday, We Will Wear Blue"

Poem-a-Day: "Wake Up, Mario," "Breve Pausa"

Poetry: "Love Song of the Bat with Vertigo," "He Could Sing, But He Couldn't Fly," "The Monster in the Lake"

Poetry Daily: "The Iguanas Skitter Through the Cemetery by the Sea"

Poetry London: "A Busload of Screaming Children"

Portside: "Big Bird Died for Your Sins"

Prairie Schooner: "The Lights That Burn in the House of Many Rooms," "I Must Be the Steamship Morro Castle," "Love Song of the Plátanos Maduros"

The Progressive: "The Puerto Rican with the Bolshevik Name"

Rejected Lit: "Moderation"

Siglo22: "The Iguanas Skitter Through the Cemetery by the Sea"

Tikkun: "The Bastard Son of King Levinsky"

Virginia Quarterly Review: "Look at This," "Big Bird Died for Your Sins," "Love Song of the Disembodied Head in a Jar," "Award Ceremony Nightmare with Swedish Meatballs," "Isabela's Red Dress Flutters Away," "The Iguanas Skitter Through the Cemetery by the Sea," "The Snake"

The Yale Review: "Banquo's Ghost in Paterson"

Many thanks to Hannah Aizenman, Julia Alvarez, JJ Amawaro Wilson, Doug Anderson, Benjamin Balthaser, Dennis Bernstein, Daniel Borzutzky, Jill Brevik, Cyrus Cassells, Sandra Cisneros, Gisela Conn, Candace Curran, Suzanne Daly, Kwame Dawes, Carlina Duan, Andre Dubus III, Cornelius Eady, Lauren Marie Espada, Chloé Firetto-Toomey, John Freeman, Gustavo Gelpí, Maria Mazziotti Gillan, Angel Guadalupe, Daniel Halpern, Le Hinton, Everett Hoagland, A. Van Jordan, Lawrence Joseph, Ilya Kaminsky, Wayne Karlin, Rebecca Kemble, Eileen Mariani, Paul Mariani, David Masciotra, Adrian Matejka, Khaled Mattawa, Katie McDonough, Rob McQuilkin, Richard Michelson, Joseph Morra, John Murillo, Mazen Naous, Joyce Carol Oates, Cindy Juyoung Ok, Gregory Pardlo, Piper Perabo, Willie Perdomo, Camilo Pérez-Bustillo, Robert Pinsky, Marcus Rediker, Jay Rose, Allen Ruff, César Salgado, Luke Salisbury, Oscar Sarmiento, Jeremy Schraffenberger, Rob Shapiro, Leslie Shipman, Victoria Silva, Gary Soto, Steve Stern, Luis Alberto Urrea, Wilson Valentín-Escobar, Rich Villar, Eleanor Wilner, Melissa Yoon, and Kevin Young.

Many thanks also to the *Virginia Quarterly Review* for their 2022 Emily Clark Balch Prize, and to Mass Humanities for their 2024 Governor's Award in the Humanities.

NOTES ON THE POEMS

My wife, Lauren Marie Espada, is the teacher in "Gonzo," "Banquo's Ghost in Paterson," "Isabela's Red Dress Flutters Away," and "On Friday, We Will Wear Blue." She is also the "Beloved" in "My Beloved the Unbeliever" and "My Beloved the Blasphemer Causes a Scuffle at the Bar." I wrote the "Love Songs" for her.

Jailbreak of Sparrows: "*Claridad*" or "clarity," refers to the socialist weekly newspaper in Puerto Rico. "Ay bendito" means "oh blessed," a common Puerto Rican expression signifying anything from pity to anger. A "bolero" is a slow, romantic ballad. "The words a poet wrote . . . to praise his beloved at the jailhouse door" alludes to Juan Antonio Corretjer and his poem "Distancias" ("Distances"), adapted as a song by Roy Brown and sung at the *Claridad* Festival. The "Partido Popular Democrático" (PPD) is the political party supporting the colonial status of Commonwealth or "Free Associated State." "Muñoz Marín . . ." is Luis Muñoz Marín, cofounder of the PPD, president of the Senate (1941–1949) and governor (1949–1965). "Pan, Tierra, Libertad" ("Bread, Land, Freedom") refers to the original party slogan of the PPD. "Jalda arriba" ("Up the Hill") refers to the official party campaign song of the PPD. Public Law 53, "La Ley de la Mordaza" ("The Law of the Muzzle" or "Gag Law") was legislation, based on the federal Smith Act and passed in June 1948 at the behest of Muñoz Marín, to silence pro-independence opposition, ranging from publication of poems to singing of songs and possession of the Puerto Rican flag, felonies punishable by imprisonment. "The 30th of October, / 1950" is the date of the Nationalist Party revolutionary uprising in towns such as "Jayuya, Arecibo, Naranjito, Utuado." The National Guard machine-gunned unarmed Nationalist prisoners in what would be called "La Masacre de Utuado" or the "Utuado Massacre." "The liberator Betances" refers to Dr. Ramón Emeterio Betances, the revolutionary who fomented an insurrection against the Spanish in 1868. "The poet who knew the room of stone" is Corretjer; "the poet new / to the room of stone" is Francisco Matos Paoli, who suffered a breakdown. More than three thousand people were arrested. The poem has its genesis in conversations with my cousin Gisela Conn and the photograph by my father, Frank Espada, "Utuado, 1967." The poem also draws upon *The Disenchanted Island: Puerto Rico and the United States in the Twentieth Century,* 2nd edition, by Ronald Fernandez (Praeger, 1996); *War Against All Puerto Ricans: Revolution and Terror in America's Colony* by Nelson Denis (Nation Books, 2015); and *La insurrección nacionalista en Puerto Rico, 1950* by Miñi Seijo Bruno (Editorial Edil, 1989).

My Father's Practice Book: Frank Espada (1930–2014) was a documentary photographer and the creator of the Puerto Rican Diaspora Documentary Project, a photo documentary and oral history of the Puerto Rican migration. The project resulted in more than forty solo exhibitions and a book entitled *The Puerto Rican Diaspora: Themes in the Survival of a People* (2006). His work is included in the collections of the Smithsonian National Museum of American History, the Smithsonian American Art Museum, the National Portrait Gallery, and the Library of Congress. "*El hijo de Frank*" ("the son of Frank") was a term applied to me well into adulthood.

Big Bird Died for Your Sins: Roberto Clemente (1934–1972) was one of the greatest players in the history of baseball, still lionized in Puerto Rico. The Baseball Writers' Association of America elected Clemente to the National Baseball Hall of Fame in March 1973, following his death in a plane crash delivering relief supplies to earthquake survivors in Nicaragua. "Guardia Nacional" refers to Nicaragua's National Guard, essentially a private army for dictator Anastasio Somoza. "His compañero the catcher" refers to Manny Sanguillén, the Panamanian catcher for the Pittsburgh Pirates.

The Lights That Burn in the House of Many Rooms: "Pernil" refers to Puerto Rican roast pork. "Mrs. Grant" is Inga Grant, an immigrant from Jamaica victimized by a cross burning in Valley Stream, Long Island. The fifth stanza draws from two articles by Shawn Kennedy in *The New York Times*: "A Cross Is Burned in Valley Stream on Lawn of Black Family's Home," August 15, 1979, and "L.I Village Trying to Forget Cross-Burning," September 20, 1979. Amerigo Vespucci was arrested for the murder of Richard Hogan and wanted for the cross burning. See "Police Bust 1979 'Killer' at Brother's Funeral Wake" by Kieran Crowley in the *New York Post,* January 19, 2002.

The Bastard Son of King Levinsky: King Levinsky, born Harris Kraków, was a contender in boxing's heavyweight division during the 1930s. He fought an exhibition with former champion Jack Dempsey, as well as bouts with future champions Primo Carnera and Joe Louis. Louis knocked out Levinsky in one round at Comiskey Park in 1935. The poem draws upon two sources of Levinsky lore: "Happy King Levinsky Day" by Pete Ehrmann on Boxing.com, April 24, 2018, and "From the Vault of Art Shay: The Story of Kingfish Levinsky" by Art Shay on Chicagoist.com, October 5, 2011. Herbert Wilens was a boxer from Gaithersburg, Maryland, called "The Hebrew Hitter." As a middleweight, he fought from 1979 to 1983 and in 1989, winning eleven bouts, losing five, and drawing one. The "Puerto Rican fighter from Jersey City" is Mark Medal, who would become light middleweight champion. "Roger the Dodger" is Roger Leonard; see "Leonard Beats Wilens in Successful 'Games' " by Dennis Collins in *The Washington Post,* March 20, 1982.

El Tiante Spins Like a Stop Sign in a Hurricane: Luis Tiant Jr., or "El Tiante," was born in Marianao, La Habana, Cuba, in 1940 and died in Wells, Maine, in 2024. His 229 wins, 49 shutouts, 2,416 strikeouts, four twenty-win seasons, and 3.30 earned run average make a case for inclusion in baseball's Hall of Fame. On August 6, 1978, I saw him pitch a shutout for the Boston Red Sox over the Milwaukee Brewers at Milwaukee's County Stadium. His father, Luis Tiant Sr., or "Señor Skinny," also from La Habana, pitched for various teams in Latin America and the Negro Leagues, including the New York Cubans. Sixto Lezcano was a Gold Glove–winning right fielder for the Brewers known for his throwing arm, leading the American League in assists in 1978. "Bella Ciao" ("Goodbye Beautiful") is a traditional Italian folk song adopted, according to legend, by the partisans who rose up against Benito Mussolini during World War II, and has become an antifascist anthem.

Better Than Stealing a Necklace of Bullets: "My history professor" was Herbert Hill (1924–2004), former National Labor Director of the NAACP and a mentor at the University of Wisconsin. WORT-FM is the listener-sponsored community radio station in Madison, Wisconsin. "Los Madrugadores" (The Early Risers) is the name of the Spanish-language morning program serving migrant families in the area, named in turn for a popular musical group in Los Angeles during the 1930s.

Guadalupe's First-Year Law School Tumbao: "Guadalupe" is Angel Anthony Guadalupe, a fellow graduate of Northeastern University Law School and a criminal defense attorney in Boston. "Tumbao," derived from "tumbar," refers to the basic rhythmic pattern played on the conga drum in Afro-Cuban or salsa music. "Tumbao" also refers to personal style, walk, presence, or character. See Bobby Sanabria's video "Playing the Congas and Tumbao, Part I," in Jazz at Lincoln Center's Jazz Academy series. Ray Barretto was a New York Puerto Rican conga drummer and bandleader in the genres of bugalú, Latin jazz, and salsa. "Que viva la música" ("Long Live the Music") was the title song of his 1972 album and was featured on his album *Tomorrow: Barretto Live* in 1976. "Salsa" is based on Afro-Cuban song forms as developed by Puerto Rican musicians in New York during the 1960s and '70s. "¿Cómo está, bróder?" is a typical combination of Spanish and English: "How are you, brother?"

The City Wears a Coat to Bed: From 1987 to 1993, I served as Supervisor of Su Clínica Legal, a legal services program for low-income, Spanish-speaking tenants in Chelsea, Massachusetts, near Boston.

Your Card Is the King of Rats: Tenant lawyer Jay Rose served as the Managing Attorney for the Housing Unit at Greater Boston Legal Services (GBLS) for many years. GBLS loaned office space in Chelsea to Su Clínica Legal. Together, we raised funds for our programs — referred to here to as "Legal Aid" — by appealing for donations from the private bar in Boston.

He Could Sing, but He Couldn't Fly: Boxer "Two-Ton" Tony Galento was a heavyweight contender in the 1930s and '40s. In the film *On the Waterfront* (1954), playing a thug for a labor racketeer, he spoke the line "He could sing, but he couldn't fly." The sentence originated with newspaper coverage of Abe Reles, a hitman for "Murder Inc." turned government informant, who allegedly fell from a window at the Half Moon Hotel in Coney Island, Brooklyn, in 1941, despite police protection. Reles was due to testify in the trial of organized crime boss Albert Anastasia. My mother, growing up in Brooklyn, was ten at the time; she would tell me this story.

The Janitor Who Swept Where There Was No Dust: "Pinochet" refers to General Augusto Pinochet, among the leaders of the 1973 coup in Chile, and the dictator of that country from 1973 to 1990.

Banquo's Ghost in Paterson: "Never shake thy gory locks at me" comes from William Shakespeare's *Macbeth* (3.4 61–62). Macbeth speaks to Banquo, who appears as a ghost at Macbeth's banquet after being murdered at his command. Ralph Dennison attended Passaic County Community College. The fourth stanza relies in part on "24-Year-Old City Man Shot to Death on Rosa Parks Boulevard" by Jonathan Greene in the *Paterson Times*, April 15, 2014.

Isabela's Red Dress Flutters Away: "Isabela" is a pseudonym. "Flaca" is "skinny woman," used here as a nickname. "The play they saw on DVD, where the white boy spat . . ." refers to *"Master Harold" . . . and the boys*, by South African playwright Athol Fugard.

Love Song of the Polar Bear Mascot at McCoy Stadium in Pawtucket, Rhode Island: The Pawtucket Red Sox (or "PawSox") served as the AAA farm team of the Boston Red Sox from 1973 to 2020, playing at McCoy Stadium in Pawtucket, Rhode Island.

Love Song of the Plátanos Maduros: Plátanos maduros, fried ripe plantains, serve as a food staple throughout the Caribbean. The "stain" refers to a common expression — "mancha de plátano" — indicative of strong Puerto Rican identity.

Love Song of Frankenstein's Insomniac Monster: The second stanza is based in part on the film *Bride of Frankenstein* (1935), with Boris Karloff as the Monster and Elsa Lanchester as the Bride.

Love Song of the Disembodied Head in a Jar: "Arroz con pollo" is chicken with rice.

I Must Be the Steamship Morro Castle: On September 8, 1934, the steamship *Morro Castle* — named for the fortress in La Habana, Cuba — caught fire off the coast of New Jersey, costing the lives of 137 crew and passengers. The ship ran aground close to shore in Asbury Park, New Jersey, where the wreck remained for months and became a tourist attraction. The second stanza relies in part on "Shore Residents Recall Fire on *Morro Castle* 40 Years Ago" by Joseph Deitch in *The New York Times,* September 8, 1974, and *Inferno at Sea: Stories of Death and Survival Aboard the* Morro Castle by Gretchen Coyle and Deborah Whitcraft (Down the Shore Publishing, 2012).

Award Ceremony Nightmare with Swedish Meatballs: I had this dream in the week preceding the National Book Award ceremony in November 2021.

Florencia, Again and Again: Steve Stern is a professor emeritus, and mentor of mine, in the History Department at the University of Wisconsin–Madison. He has published *Remembering Pinochet's Chile: On the Eve of London 1998* (Duke University Press, 2004); *Battling for Hearts and Minds: Memory Struggles in Pinochet's Chile, 1973–1988* (Duke University Press, 2006); and *Reckoning with Pinochet: The Memory Question in Democratic Chile, 1989–2006* (Duke University Press, 2010). Florencia Mallón is a professor emerita in the History Department at the University of Wisconsin–Madison. She is the author of *Peasant and Nation: The Making of Postcolonial México and Perú* (University of California Press, 1995); *When a Flower Is Reborn: The Life and Times of a Mapuche Feminist* (Duke University Press, 2002); and *Courage Tastes of Blood: The Mapuche Community of Nicolás Ailío and the Chilean State, 1906–2001* (Duke University Press, 2005). Stern and Mallón married in 1978. The second stanza quotes "Gracias a la vida" ("Thanks to Life"), composed by Chilean singer-songwriter Violeta Parra (1917–1967). The poem is based on conversations with Steve Stern and Rebecca Kemble of the Threshold Singers of Madison.

Insult: William Carlos Williams (1883–1963) was one of the twentieth century's most important poets. An advocate for the "American idiom," he received the first National Book Award in

Poetry in 1950 and the Pulitzer Prize (posthumously) in 1963. He was also a practicing physician in Rutherford and Paterson, New Jersey, for four decades. In August 1952, Williams suffered a stroke that left his upper right side paralyzed. He retired from medicine and spent two months hospitalized for depression, from mid-February to mid-April 1953. His appointment as Consultant in Poetry to the Library of Congress — the equivalent of today's Poet Laureate — was revoked following an FBI investigation into false charges that he was a communist. The organizations, affiliations, and publications in the second stanza come from the poet's declassified FBI file. The "demagogue" who accused Williams of riding the "I Love Russia Trolley" was columnist and radio personality Fulton Lewis Jr. in his "Washington Report," November 21, 1952. The quotation in the third stanza comes from an unpublished postcard sent by Williams to Swarthmore College. "It is difficult / to get the news from poems . . ." comes from "Asphodel, That Greeny Flower" in *Journey to Love* (Random House, 1955). The poem began with the postcard, but conversations and emails with biographer Paul Mariani were invaluable, along with Mariani's *William Carlos Williams: A New World Naked* (McGraw-Hill, 1981). See also "William Carlos Williams (1883–1963): Physician-Writer and 'Godfather of Avant-Garde Poetry'" by Dr. Richard Carter in *The Annals of Thoracic Surgery,* 67 (5): 1512–17, 1999.

The Fireflies of Belmont Avenue: Jules Chametzky (1928–2021) was a colleague in the English Department at the University of Massachusetts–Amherst. Chametzky cofounded *The Massachusetts Review,* coedited *Jewish American Literature: A Norton Anthology* (W. W. Norton, 2000), and published a "cultural memoir," *Out of Brownsville: Encounters with Nobel Laureates and Other Jewish Writers* (Meredith Winter Press, 2012). I wrote this poem for a symposium entitled "The Legacy of Jules Chametzky" at the University of Massachusetts–Amherst, October 7, 2022.

My Debs, My Eugene: Eugene Victor Povirk (1948–2022) was a bookseller and proprietor of Southpaw Books in Conway, Massachusetts. A draft resister during the war in Vietnam, Povirk was named after Eugene Victor Debs, union leader, pacifist, socialist, orator, and presidential candidate of the Socialist Party. The poem quotes the statement by Debs at his sentencing hearing after being convicted of sedition for a speech against the draft in 1918. Debs ran for president from prison in 1920 and received nearly a million votes; campaign buttons read, "For President Prisoner No. 9653." In the fourth stanza, "who shot the poet in a flophouse" refers to Maxwell Bodenheim and his murder; "who led the strikers in the singing" refers to John Reed and the Paterson Silk Strike; "who died of drink to leave the books she loved in her husband's chilly mansion" refers to Louise Bryant and her marriage to William Bullitt. "The artist charged with sedition" is Art Young, a defendant in *The Masses* trials. The first stanza draws upon *Eugene V. Debs: Citizen and Socialist* by Nick Salvatore (University of Illinois Press, 1982).

The Puerto Rican with the Bolshevik Name: Vladimir Morales (1951–2022) was born in Dorado, Puerto Rico. He was a community activist and member of the School Committee in Amherst, Massachusetts. An appointee of President Warren Harding, Emmet Montgomery Reily was the governor of Puerto Rico from 1921 to 1923. The quotation of Reily comes from his inaugural address. This stanza relies in part on *Prisoners of Colonialism: The Struggle for Justice in Puerto Rico* by Ronald Fernandez (Common Courage Press, 1994). I read this poem when Morales posthumously received the Jean Haggerty Award for Community Engagement and Social Justice, with his wife, Victoria Silva, from Amherst Media, November 18, 2023.

The Last Words of Hurricane Hi: Hiram Gabriel Bithorn Sosa (1916–1951) was the first Puerto Rican player in the major leagues. As a pitcher for the Chicago Cubs in 1943, he won eighteen games with a 2.60 earned run average, and seven shutouts to lead the National League. He was attempting a comeback in the Mexican League when police officer Ambrosio Castillo-Cano shot and killed Bithorn in El Mante, México, on December 29, 1951. Witnesses saw Chief of Police Fidel Garza driving Bithorn's car afterward. Castillo-Cano was convicted of homicide and received an eight-year sentence. The poem draws upon several sources for the fragmented story: "Hi Bithorn: Puerto Rico's Baseball Pioneer" by Andrew Martin, on Seamheads.com, January 20, 2012; "Hi Bithorn" by Jane Allen-Quevedo in *Puerto Rico and Baseball: 60 Biographies,* edited by Bill Nowlin and Edwin Fernández (Society for American Baseball Research, 2017); and *Sobre la vida de Hiram Gabriel Bithorn Sosa* by Jorge Fidel López Vélez (Extreme Graphic Incorporated, 2016).

Officer Mark Dial, Who Shot Eddie Irizarry, Will Be Fired for Insubordination: On August 14, 2023, Philadelphia police officer Mark Dial shot Eddie Irizarry, who was sitting in his car with the windows rolled up, six times. Dial and his partner reported that Irizarry fled a traffic stop, emerged from the car, and lunged at them with a knife. A doorbell home surveillance video proved otherwise. Chief of Police Danielle Outlaw fired Dial because he refused to cooperate. Dial has been charged with third-degree murder, and the family has filed a wrongful death claim. The fourth stanza relies on the surveillance video, and the poem as a whole draws upon a series of articles by Ellie Rushing and Rodrigo Torrejón in *The Philadelphia Inquirer*: "Man Killed by Philadelphia Police Never Got out of His Car, Didn't 'Lunge' with a Knife, Police Say in New Narrative," August 16, 2023; "New Video Shows Philadelphia Police Officer Shot Eddie Irizarry Within Seconds of Getting out of Patrol Car," August 22, 2023; "Officer Mark Dial, Who Shot Eddie Irizarry, Will Be Fired for Insubordination, Outlaw Says," August 23, 2023; and "Friends and Loved Ones Gather for the Funeral of Eddie Irizarry, Shot and Killed by a Philadelphia Police Officer," August 24, 2023.

Wake Up, Mario: Mario González Arenales (1994–2021), from Oakland, California, died after being pinned facedown for five minutes by three Alameda police officers on April 19, 2021. An independent autopsy found that González died from "restraint asphyxiation." In December 2023, the city of Alameda settled wrongful death claims on behalf of González's seven-year-old son and mother for $11.4 million. The officers have been charged with involuntary manslaughter. Bodycam video showed that González was neither armed nor verbally or physically threatening. One officer kept a knee in his upper back till González became unresponsive. This homicide occurred on the same day jury deliberations began in the trial of officer Derek Chauvin, who pinned George Floyd down with a knee to the neck for more than nine minutes in May 2020 and was convicted of murder in Minneapolis. "Salem's Puritan Days" and "More weight" refer to Giles Corey, the farmer pressed to death during the Salem Witch Trials. "Crucita" is a pseudonym. The poem draws upon the bodycam video and relies in part on "Alameda Releases Video Showing Police Pinning Mario Gonzalez to Ground Before His Death" by David Debolt and George Kelly in *The Mercury News,* April 27, 2021; "California Man Dies After Police Pin Him to Ground for 5 Minutes" by Will Wright in *The New York Times,* April 27, 2021; and "Bodycam Video Shows California Man Who Died After Officers Pinned Him to Ground for 5 Minutes" by Sophie Lewis, CBS News, April 29, 2021.

The Faces We Envision in the Scrapbook of the Dead: Camilo Pérez-Bustillo is an international human rights lawyer and former Executive Director of the National Lawyers Guild–San Francisco Bay Area chapter. He also served as Advocacy Director for the Hope Border Institute in El Paso, Texas, and was instrumental in the closing of the migrant adolescent internment camp in nearby Tornillo, along with Joshua Rubin, "the solitary man" with the sign that says, "Free Them." On August 3, 2019, Patrick Wood Crusius, armed with a semiautomatic rifle, killed twenty-three people and wounded twenty-two more at the Walmart near the Cielo Vista Mall in El Paso. The poem quotes from the anti-immigrant manifesto posted to the message board 8chan by Crusius proving that he targeted Latinos. He pleaded guilty to federal hate crimes charges and was sentenced to ninety consecutive life terms. "Arturo" is Arturo Benavides, who was sixty when he died in the mass shooting. The poem draws upon conversations and emails with Pérez-Bustillo, as well as his article "The El Paso Attack Was Not Just a Mass Shooting. It was a Genocidal Massacre," in *Truthout,* August 14, 2021.

The Snake: At certain rallies since his 2016 campaign for president, Donald Trump has read the lyrics of a song — which he calls a "poem" — entitled "The Snake," misattributed by him to Al Wilson but written and recorded by Oscar Brown Jr. in 1963. Brown was a singer, songwriter, poet, and civil rights activist. He based "The Snake" on Aesop's fable "The Farmer and the Viper." The second stanza is based in part on the Woodlands Online "Trump 'Save America' Rally Conroe TX 22 Photo Gallery." The third stanza summarizes and quotes the song used by Trump as an anti-immigrant parable; Brown's family asked Trump to stop using it. "The millionaire who sells / pillows" is Michael Lindell, CEO of MyPillow. A Department of Labor investigation into the use of underage labor on the cleaning crews of slaughterhouses — including JBS in Grand Island, Nebraska — revealed more than one hundred such cases in eight states, for which Packers Sanitation Services paid $1.5 million in fines. The Trump quotes come from the Save America rally in Conroe, Texas, on January 29, 2022, where he read "The Snake," covered by C-SPAN. The fourth stanza draws upon the CBS program *60 Minutes* entitled "This Ancient Atrocity," May 7, 2023, and "'They Were Little': Photos Show Children Illegally Working in US Slaughterhouse" by Lauren Aratani in *The Guardian,* May 9, 2023.

Breve Pausa: Juan Antonio Corretjer (1908–1985) was a major poet and advocate for independence in Puerto Rico. He was imprisoned multiple times for his writings, speeches, and organizing on behalf of the independence cause. His wife, Consuelo Lee Tapia (1905–1989), was also a writer and activist for independence. In 1969, they were charged with conspiracy; in 1971, they were incarcerated. The charges were ultimately dismissed. An uncredited photograph captured the moment when they kissed goodbye prior to being taken away to their respective prisons at Castillo de Ponce and Vega Alta. This photograph appears on the cover of Corretjer's poetry book *Pausa para el amor (Pause for Love),* published in the 1976 edition by the Instituto de Cultura Puertorriqueña. The quotations in the last stanza come from his poem "El Convoy." "Despedida" is "farewell." "The mountain town" is Ciales.

The Iguanas Skitter Through the Cemetery by the Sea: The poem is based on a visit to the Cementerio Santa María Magdalena de Pazzis in Viejo San Juan, Puerto Rico, in August, 2022. There was an island-wide infestation of iguanas at the time. José de Diego (1866–1918) was a poet, lawyer, political leader in the House of Delegates, and advocate of independence. The two quotations in the second stanza come from his anticolonial poems "Al guaraguao" ("To the Hawk") and "¡Pitirre!" ("Kingbird!") in *Cantos de Pitirre* (*Songs of the Kingbird*), Instituto de Literatura Puertorriqueña, 1949. The poet utilizes a saying in Puerto Rico: "Cada guaraguao tiene su pitirre" ("Every hawk has his kingbird"), based on the kingbird's fierce defense of the nest against the hawk. Pedro Albizu Campos (1893–1965) was a lawyer, organizer, orator, president of the Nationalist Party, and revolutionary leader of the independence movement in Puerto Rico. His oratory earned him the honorific "El Maestro" ("The Teacher"). "The cane cutters' strike" alludes to the labor stoppage led by Albizu in 1934. "Thirty years' incarceration" refers to Albizu's convictions for "seditious conspiracy," which kept him incarcerated for most of the period between 1936 and his death in 1965. *The Lost World* is the 1960 film based on the Arthur Conan Doyle novel of the same name.

A NOTE ABOUT THE AUTHOR

MARTÍN ESPADA has published more than twenty books as a poet, editor, essayist, and translator. His previous book of poems, *Floaters,* won the 2021 National Book Award, as well as the Massachusetts Book Award, and was a finalist for the *Los Angeles Times* Book Prize. Other books of poems include *Vivas to Those Who Have Failed* (2016), *The Trouble Ball* (2011), *The Republic of Poetry* (2006), *Alabanza* (2003), and *Imagine the Angels of Bread* (1996). He is the editor of *What Saves Us: Poems of Empathy and Outrage in the Age of Trump* (2019). He has received the Ruth Lilly Poetry Prize, the Shelley Memorial Award, the Robert Creeley Award, an Academy of American Poets Fellowship, the PEN/Revson Fellowship, a Letras Boricuas Fellowship, and a Guggenheim Fellowship. *The Republic of Poetry* was a finalist for the Pulitzer Prize. The title poem of his collection *Alabanza,* about 9/11, has been widely anthologized and performed. His book of essays and poems, *Zapata's Disciple* (1998), was banned in Tucson as part of the Mexican American Studies Program outlawed by the state of Arizona. A former tenant lawyer in Greater Boston, Espada is a professor of English at the University of Massachusetts–Amherst.

A NOTE ABOUT THE TYPE

This book was set in Agmena, which was designed by Jovica Veljović for Linotype in 2012. Inspired by the forms and proportions of Renaissance fonts, Veljović created Agmena with the intent of making the perfect text face for books. Agmena was awarded a Certificate of Typographic Excellence by the Type Directors Club in 2013.

Composed by North Market Street Graphics
Lancaster, Pennsylvania

Designed by Marisa Nakasone